SEEN
IN SURREY

by Chris Howkins

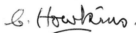

PUBLISHED BY CHRIS HOWKINS

Balleshall
C. Howkins 1991

FOR GORDON
IN APPRECIATION OF
TEN YEARS OF GUIDANCE

First published 1993

© Chris Howkins

A Howkins-Hemsley production
Published By Chris Howkins,
70 Grange Road, New Haw,
Addlestone, Surrey, KT15 3RH

Printed in England by Ian Allan Printing Ltd.,
Coombelands House, Coombelands Lane,
Addlestone, Surrey, KT15 1HY

ISBN   0 9519348 4 8

Surrey Advertiser Ltd

Directors:
R. S. Tindle, C.B.E., *Chairman*
I. G. McEwan
J. S. Tucker, *Secretary*
P. M. Windsor-Aubrey

Head Office:
P.O. Box 20
Martyr Road
Guildford, Surrey
GU1 4LQ
Telephone: 0483 571234
Facsimile: 0483 32843
AD-DOC: DX 2452
GUILDFORD

I, on behalf of the Surrey Advertiser, am delighted to have been asked to contribute a Foreword to this celebration of 10 years of Seen in Surrey articles by Chris Howkins.

The decade has passed quickly. During it, Chris Howkins has established himself as one of the county's leading authorities on local history and its flora and fauna.

We, at the newspaper, like to think that we helped him to get his name more widely known. It was my predecessor as editor, the late Ted Adams, who gave Chris the opportunity to have a regular platform in the Surrey Advertiser. And, encouraged by Gordon Weaver, then a senior member of the editorial staff, Chris began to put down the marker that was to enable him to build up a large following of devoted readers.

His well researched articles, with their accompanying drawings, were eagerly awaited, and they soon began to lead to other things.

It was only natural, therefore, that after 10 years of Seen in Surrey he would find the time in his busy schedule to publish a collection of his writings and drawings that have delighted our readers since 1983.

Graham Collyer
Editor, Surrey Advertiser

Registered No. 1241000 England. Registered Office: Advertiser House, Martyr Road, Guildford, Surrey.

EDITOR'S INTRODUCTION

This volume is a selection of the features written and illustrated by Chris Howkins, published by the Surrey Advertiser over the last ten years. The venture started back in 1983 when his 'Doorstep Book' was spotted by the newspaper's chief sub-editor, Gordon Weaver. His interest led to an introduction to Chris Howkins, resulting with a meeting with the then editor of the Surrey Advertiser, Ted Adams.

Mr. Adams commissioned six features, of no more than 500 words each, to run fortnightly. So the Surrey Advertiser coined the logo 'Seen in Surrey', sought to change Christopher to Chris, which has stuck ever since, and the series began. The readership response was such that after the six features, the arrangement was extended 'indefinitely'. In due course Mr. Adams retired and his successor, Graham Collyer, retained the features and did so again recently when the paper was redesigned.

After ten years there have been 245 features and it has been a difficult task to extract the most memorable. It was decided from the outset to choose from those featuring the people and places that have a lasting value in the county, ruling out the wildlife and topical features. Here the original text has been used, before editing to suit the newspaper and so, here too is the original setting of the illustrations which have, in some cases been kept available in other books. Some features had to be omitted because the picture has been sold without a photocopy being retained while in some cases a different picture has been substituted or the original improved with the finer detail that would not have reproduced well on newsprint. The features have been set in chronological order so that all the anniversaries follow in correct sequence, with the original date of publication provided at the end.

D.R.Hemsley

ACKNOWLEDGEMENTS

I should like to thank the people at the Surrey Advertiser, past and present, for all their help and encouragement, and, to all the hundreds of readers who, one way or another, have helped to make the series a success. I can remember only two occasions when a proposed feature was 'blocked', although there has been quite a fuss over several! I am greatly indebted to Darren Hemsley for undertaking the enormous task of creating this book and to Sue Harvey for working with him to process the text. The work involved in getting the features to fit the pages, in a hand-made book, is considerable, and I am very appreciative of their patience, determination and effort.

C. Howkins

GENERAL GORDON

I've just walked past China, seen a camel, and listened for the pipes and drums. It's just another Friday in Surrey, at Gordon's School, West End.

Today, January 26th, is special for them, beginning with a wreath-laying service at the school, followed (for some) by a second service on London's Embankment before the statue of General Charles Gordon who died on this day in 1885.

He was one of our great generals, sent by Gladstone's Government to evacuate Egyptian forces from Khartoum during the Mahdi's Revolt. He endured a ten month siege while waiting for our government to take positive action but it let him down. He was killed shortly before the arrival of the relief force. Queen Victoria broke down in tears.

She insisted upon a memorial and the world agreed. Money arrived from far and wide to fund an international memorial to a great leader. Two portraits of him look down from the headmaster's study walls, looking definitely Victorian and military and yet both artists caught a softness of humanity in the eyes and countenance.

Thus it was (eventually) decided that the memorial should perpetuate the humanitarian rather than the soldier and it was this boarding school, for 'necessitous lads' that won final approval. The Gordon School (now co-educational) was at first on Portsdown Hill overlooking Portsmouth, until the present Chobham site was ready - fifty acres leased from the War Department.

The boarding houses make an impressive grouping round a long quadrangle. There is 'China' to commemorate 'Chinese' Gordon's command of the Chinese forces against the rebel Taipings (1863-4). His yellow mandarin's costume is still a prize possession of the school museum which contains the largest collection of memorabilia.

There's another called 'Gravesend', where Gordon developed his interests in helping disadvantaged children, and also 'Woolwich' where he was born, and of course 'Khartoum' where he was betrayed and died.

(26.1 90)

COMMEMORATING SAMUEL PALMER

Sheep are wonderful, textured creatures to draw. The agent's sale particulars of a house at Box Hill claim that it was lived in by one of Britain's most individual artists who imbued sheepy landscapes with a special magic. He was Samuel Palmer, born on this day, January 27th, in 1805 and who spent the last twenty years of his life in the Redhill area.

Here Palmer rose to the peak of his artistic career, achieving a near perfect balance between his inner deeply Christian vision and his sharply observed outward vision. Sadly these powers were fading by about 1832 and in 1835 he left Shoreham to begin a new phase.

By the time he arrived he had passed his artistic peak. He'd begun early, exhibiting at the Royal Academy while still only fourteen. He wanted painting lessons though and turned to the artist John Linnell, who remained his life-long associate and even outlived him by a year.

Linnell told him to study the works of Albrecht Durer and Lucas Van Leyden which he did and took from them his hard lines, clear forms and those marvellous rich textures. He also fell under the spell of William Blake and met the great man at Linnell's house at Hampstead - quite a day as Blake hated Hampstead.

Ill health prompted Palmer to leave London for Shoreham, in Kent, the next year and there he started attracting other artists to his home. They were much taken with Blake's notion that Ancient Man was a nobler being than his modern counterpart. They called themselves The Ancients and provoked local censure of their behaviour and dress but attracted Blake himself to visit them, the year before his death.

He married the daughter of Linnell who thus became an important influence again. By 1850 Linnell's own success enabled him to buy land out in the country - at Redhill. It has since been built over as Redstone Hill, hence Linnell Road. Thus the Palmers came to Bell Street, Reigate, to a house opposite the Priory Park, before moving to Furze Hill House off Linkfield Lane, where Furze Hill Road has been built.

Linnell changed. He drove Palmer to produce work in a commercial style and the former glories were never seen again. The beautiful sheepy downs all along the back of their home no longer worked their magic.

Palmer died in 1881 and was buried in the cemetery of St Mary's, Reigate.

(27.1.89)

10

RESTORING VICTORIAN HASCOMBE

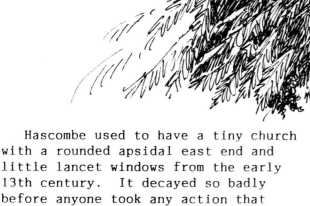

Hascombe Brewey

Hascombe used to have a tiny church with a rounded apsidal east end and little lancet windows from the early 13th century. It decayed so badly before anyone took any action that there were trees growing out of the roof. The best solution was to demolish it and start again.

The work was entrusted to one of Surrey's greater architects, Henry Woodyer. His work was rather variable but fortunately this commission seems to have appealed and he produced his finest church in the county, and one of his best anywhere.

He modelled the new and much larger building on the 13th century original, complete with rounded apse, and at the same time capturing something of that special village church character. It does not simply restate what had been expressed centuries before but speaks boldly of its own culture of 1864. Thus the simplicity of the outside in no way prepares the visitor for the lavish decorations inside - from the stained glass to the great mural schemes. Even the medieval screen, saved from the old church, was brought alive again with colour and figures. It is all a complete mid-Victorian decorative scheme of quite some rarity; one which Ian Nairn in "The Buildings of England" said was "worth careful preservation."

That's what the people of Hascombe set about doing. Time had taken its toll on the paintings and so the firm of Perry Lithgow was brought in to ensure the work of the Victorian artists should live on. Who those artists were is unknown, except that there were four of them, working to the designs of a Mr Pippit, for the famous firm of Hardman and Powell, chosen by Woodyer to do the work.

Anyone who has seen the intricate scheme at Hascombe can imagine what an enormous task was the restoration. The cost doesn't bear thinking about either. The original scheme is thought to have been paid for by the incumbent, the rather notable Canon Musgrave but now the thinly-populated parish had to set about raising £50,000. The work was so important that it attracted support from Sotheby's who held a Valuation Day in Cranleigh to raise funds. By the time this feature appeared the work was half way towards completion.

(10. 2.89)

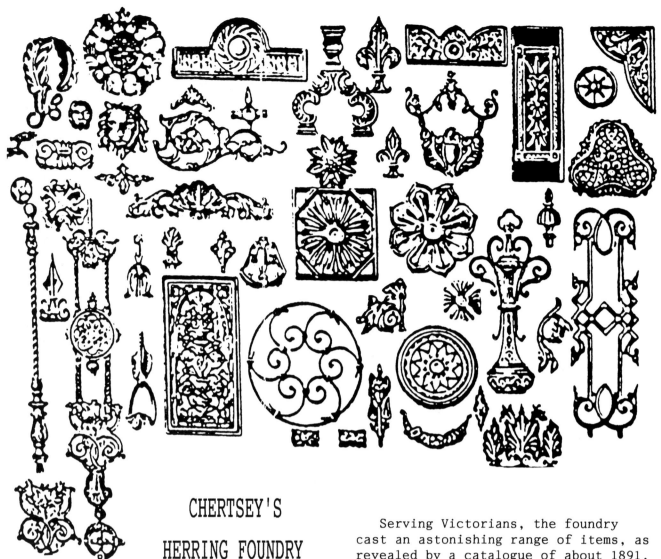

CHERTSEY'S HERRING FOUNDRY

(Adjusted from publicity for an
exhibition)

When the Fire Station in Toronto,
Canada, wanted a public clock they
chose the Herring Foundry at Chertsey
to cast the faces. The prototype is
now part of the Chertsey Museum
collections and has the Roman numerals
wrongly positioned.

Mention iron foundries in Surrey
and our minds tend to zoom back
hundreds of years to the days before
coal. Many people will no doubt be
surprised that in Chertsey town centre
the works operated until 1982. The
foundry is believed to have been
started by William Herring when he
took over the family ironmonger's
business of the death of his father,
Anthony, in 1827. Very soon he
expanded the business and took over
the old police station.

Serving Victorians, the foundry
cast an astonishing range of items, as
revealed by a catalogue of about 1891.
It contains pages and pages of
illustrations like the one reproduced
as the background to the illustration.
Castings had as much skill and care
lavished upon them whatever their
size. In particular, the company was
proud of its stoves and was one of the
few to cast its name upon them.
Another speciality was iron
conservatories after they were made
popular by the Great Exhibition of
1851. A hundred years on and the same
foundry was casting the lamp standards
for the Great Exhibition of 1951. The
enormous carved wooden patterns,
looking at first glance like ships'
cannons have survived and become part
of the museum collection.

The 15,000 sq ft site has now been
redeveloped, sweeping away not only
the industrial past but the literary
too - connections with Thomas Love
Peacock, Charles Dickens and "Oliver
Twist". The Herring collection is
normally in store rather than on
permanent display in the museum.

(12. 2.88)

THE BATTLE OF FARNHAM

The Battle of Farnham is not in the history books. It did not happen. Sir William Temple of Moor Park near Farnham was so sure it was going to happen on his estate that he fled back to his former home in London (by then home of his son). That was back in 1688. James II was king and still propounding Roman Catholicism so six lords and a bishop, independently of Parliament, invited Protestant William of Orange to come and save us from "a perpetuation of evil."

Dutch William landed at Tor Bay on November 5th and King James, a keen soldier, joined his beloved army. The confrontation was expected in West Surrey, probably on Bagshot Heath, but dear old Sir William was taking no chances. The generals, however, deserted James who then had no choice but to negotiate. The terms hinged on him abandoning his Catholic policy which he found unacceptable and so he fled to Ireland. After the Battle of the Boyne he fled into exile in France.

Thus on this day, February 13th, in 1689 William and his wife Mary were proclaimed joint monarchs with the Protestant line ensured through the Act of Settlement. Diplomat and statesman, Sir William Temple was safe at Moor Park where he continued his love of gardening.

His London gardens were famous and much visited. At Moor Park he set about creating a garden in the Dutch style, complete with a canal. Such gardens became the height of fashion especially as the new monarchs were gardening enthusiasts themselves and actively promoted the Dutch style.

The king was reputed to have "repulsive manners" which I guess means they were Dutch rather than English but they didn't deter Temple from hosting his king to visit his gardens. Several books repeat the statement that here the king showed the Dutch method of cutting asparagus to Temple's young secretary. This was Johnathan Swift, later famous for 'Gulliver's Travels' and who also caught Temple's enthusiasm for gardening. The intriguing question as to how the Dutch cut asparagus has proved difficult to answer. The staff of the Royal Horticultural Society library have proved ever helpful and suggest it refers to the design of the blade used. In England there was a choice of knives, with local names like the Cambridgeshire Knife , but in France they used a gouge so that the asparagus should be cradled in the hollow. If this was a Continental, rather than a specifically French, practice then we might have an explanation. There were, after all, strong horticultural links betwen France and Holland.

Johnathan Swift was related to the Rev'd. Thomas Swift who was incumbent of Puttenham for fifty-eight years until he died in 1752 aged eighty-six. This cleric was cousin to Sir William Temple and at Moor Park the Temple arms can still be seen cast in iron over the door but of the gardens nothing remains.

(13.2.87)

14

1890

Moor
Park
Gatehouse

15

The illustration used for the feature on
Arnold Dolmetsch (1858-1940); pioneer in
the revival of early music and in particular
of the recorder. He established workshops at
Haslemere where new instruments could be
made again, with all the fine craftsmanship
and precision required to achieve both beauty
and a true note.

LOOKING FOR THE KING

I've been to see King Edward II. It meant climbing up scaffolding in Byfleet church to join Miss Ann Balantyne who is the professional with the task of cleaning the medieval wall painting that has long been thought to represent Edward.

From stylistic and costume details it is clear the work dates from about 1280. In other words it was part of the original architecture although some people have suggested the later date of c.1310 but this now seems highly unlikely. The painting itself has always been a confusing design of lines and the reason for this is now clear. There are three phases of work on the same scene.

Firstly, some of the original marking-out lines survive, including an arc over the figure's head, suggesting a canopy was envisaged orginally but not fulfilled. Then comes the main figure. He is enthroned in a building with flying buttresses which have been lowered on the dexter side to allow for his outstretched hand. This pointed to something significant in the adjoining scene but that, alas, has not survived. The thumb was drawn raised but was painted lowered.

Quite a number of other alterations show elsewhere. These date from a later phase when the background was added. The medieval wall paintings were not intended to last for ever and it is quite regular for them to have been blocked out and a different subject painted over the top. Thus modern restorers have the difficulty of deciding which layer to keep.

At Byfleet something more interesting happened. Only a thin coat of limewash was added so that it was semi-transparent when wet and the original figure was repainted with alterations. His costume and hairstyle were updated and he was given a fashionable beard and moustache. Most significantly his left hand was lowered to his knee, implying that the adjoining scene was changed and no longer needed his gesture.

Current reading of the iconography says he was a powerful person because his legs are crossed. It used to be throught that crossed legs indicated that the subject had been on a crusade but biographical research has disproved this. Now it is thought it means a violent death. This arises from the belief that the life forces flowed up one leg and down the other. To cross the legs interrupted this flow and caused death. Thus the power of some could be emphasised by this death defying act.

Is this powerful person Edward II who lived at Byfleet Manor? It has been said that the name was painted by the side but there is no trace of it. A king was always shown crowned but this man has none and nor does he bear the kingly symbols of office - the sceptre and orb. Whoever he was he wasn't Edward II. His identity remains a mystery. All we know is that he once helped give a final message to the people of Byfleet as they turned to him in order to leave by the door beneath his feet.

(15.2.85)

MORE THAN JUST A POND

Ret is a lovely little word with
which to defeat Scrabble opponents.
It means to soak flax plants with
water till the soft tissue falls off
to leave the fibres for making linen.
That's a tricky process if the whole
lot is not to rot and so ruin the
fibres. Less obvious today is that
this was once a common skill in
Surrey. Flax was grown widely for
hundreds of years.

The very words linen and flax are
Anglo-Saxon and occurred in many
languages of north west Europe at that
time. The Frisians used the word flex
rather than flax and that is the word
that was used in Surrey, suggesting
where some of our Saxons may well have
come from. It survives in place names
like Flexford and Flexlands.

The Norse people knew about retting
too but in piecing together this long
story of linen in Surrey there has
been one great gap - where and how was
the flax retted? In general use there
were two favoured methods. One was to
spread it on grass for twenty to
thirty days and soak it with buckets
of water if it dried out, which was
known as dew retting. The second
option was to submerge it in pools of
gently running water, which was known
as water retting. With so many
streams in Surrey both options were
possible but water retting would seem
to be the more likely as it was less
labour intensive. Why pay people to
lug buckets of water when a stream
could be diverted?

I was told to look for places where
a stream bank had been hollowed out to
create a retting pool but long
searches failed to provide anything
that looked convincing. Such places
would have been in use until well into
the last century so they should still
survive, even if overgrown. The more
I looked the more I doubted that such
places ever existed, for even a single
field of flax would yield more than
could be accommodated in a bank
hollow. I needed to find something
bigger.

Ponds came under scrutiny but most
were rather small and too deep - old
marl pits, roadstone pits etc. They
needed to be bigger and shallower to
allow the harvest to be spread, turned
and checked every day. Then came a
letter which had nothing to do with
flax but the address did: Little
Flexford, at Wanborough. It's been
called that since the early 1300's so
the flax connection must have been
well established even by then. The
ford part of the name was interesting
too and on being invited to go and
look I found that the driveway did
indeed include a little stream. To
the right was a sluice into a wide
channel that fed a lovely big pool
which was obviously not just another
farmyard pond. It had been carefully
given a roughly rectangular shape and
it looked as though the depth had been
fairly constant. It did have an
island but that need not have been an
original feature.

There were sluices to let the water
out too, so the water was easily
controllable. It could be drained or
filled at will but for what purpose?
Retting flax?

(21.2.90)

18

WILLIAM COBBETT

Mild and sunny, torrential rain and coldest grey - what a week! It did give a chance to see the varying moods of an English winter, from Snowdrops foaming out of hedge bottoms to cascade down the banks of a sunken lane in West Sussex to a thin sun glowing in the mists of a furrowed field in Hampshire. It seemed like the dead of winter but back among the Surrey gardens and fields there were already many signs of approaching Spring.

Our much-loved rural pattern took much of its present form only last century following the Enclosure Acts. Many of the changes were recorded by William Cobbett in his "Rural Rides". He gives little comment to the great horse teams achieving this (or even of the continued use of oxen) for there was no other way. Now they are one of the most impressive reminders of agricultural change.

Although he was born in Surrey, at Farnham, Cobbett's political career took him far afield from the local agricultural scene he grew up to love and understand. He looked at the particular but could see it broadly - not that he's very broad-minded. He's got a fixed set of beliefs and disbeliefs, of loves and hates and prejudices, to make modern readers smile or gnash teeth.

It was in the 1820's. The agricultural workers were lowly paid and so in 1830 they rebelled. There were outbreaks of arson at Egham, Guildford, Capel and Albury. Then, on November 22nd, the Riot Act had to be read at Dorking where magistrates had been swearing in special constables. The labourers took no notice but rampaged up and down the High Street, smashing every window in the magistrates' hideout. Eleven were arrested.

The next day brought a Royal Proclamation against rioters in the southern counties and the military were called in. Soldiers guarded the gunpowder mills at Chilworth but the action moved to London and to further riots in Westminster Hall itself, leading to loss of life. The king, William IV, had problems.

Out in the country the traditions created backwardness. Cobbett had been trying to promote the growing of Swedish Turnips (Swedes) and noted carefully (August 7th 1823) what he found at Thursley. Despite him advocating the growing of them in rows the fields had been sown broadcast, with poor results. He would have had forty fits if he had known I'd be broadcasting Kale seed only a few miles away, 130 years later! We used a "fiddle" which was a cross between bagpipes and a violin. The bag was filled with seed instead of wind and this trickled down on to a fluted wheel that spun the seed off when rotated by a stringed bow. The art of even distribution rested upon a regular speed of both walking and fiddling while heading in a STRAIGHT line to a marker in the opposite hedge.

The William Cobbett from Long Bridge 1990

I was always in trouble for watching the birdlife rather than the marker. My own complaint was that my bowing arm was always ready for a tea break before the farmer's!

Cobbett, who began work as a bird scarer in the fields, was born on this day, March 9th, in 1763.

(9.3.84)

H. G. WELLS

Brick can be a beautiful and versatile building material so it is reassuring to hear that the remodelling of Woking town centre will be in brick - "the older it gets the better it looks."

They seem to have only just finished Woking's centre and now they're at it again. It must surely be Surrey's most unloved town, so maybe it is not such a bad thing although putting a roof over the whole lot has a certain ring of fantasy and the architect's drawings do look rather unbelievable. I don't have the imagination of H.G. Wells.

He moved into Maybury Road by the station in 1895 and promptly had Woking destroyed by the Martians. Not that there was much to destroy. Woking was a tiny place on the edge of the great heath and it was open heath too with clear views right up to the skyline at Ottershaw. The whole forgotten landscape comes back to life as we flee the Martians through the pages of "War of the Worlds".

After living in Sutton he delighted in his new Woking home - "A small resolute semi-detatched villa with a minute greenhouse," where he began his life-long love of gardening. He added to his diary a quick cartoon of the proud moment when he harvested his first marrow. How different he'd find it all now. Even the railways have changed, as Woking celebrates the 150th anniversary of their arrival. Wells commented that "all night long the goods trains shunted and bumped and clattered," but "without serious effect upon our healthy slumbers."

Changes were already gaining momentum in his own lifetime. The county is thick with Victorian cottages of the 1890's so that everywhere he went he must have found builders at work. It showed up when he accepted Sunday lunch with Grant Allen at Hindhead which was still a "lonely place in a great black, purple and golden wilderness."

It must have reminded him of living at Sutton which was then only twenty minutes walk from the open Downs. He enjoyed the long, long walks over the open turf up to Epsom and Banstead or right over to Dorking. How he'd hate Banstead today, smothered in the very development he deplored - "little sub-estates, red-brick villas and art cottages," condemned by him in "Mr Britling Sees it Through." Not that he objected to change - only to poor quality. People don't change much though; I love Wells' description in War of the Worlds" of the Byfleet man in a panic trying to save a wheelbarrow load of his precious orchids. I'm sure we could find Wells a couple of those characters today!

(11.3.88)

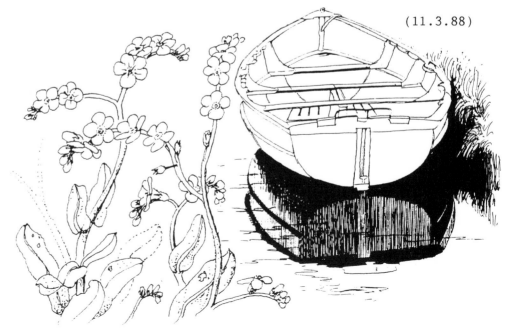

Purple Loosestrife and the Water Forget-me-Not: two of the wild flowers appreciated by H.G.Wells along the Basingstoke Canal.

WOKING
The original rough drawing;
couldn't be re-worked as the
scene has altered with the
building of the Peacocks Centre.

23

ALBURY'S DEBT TO PUGIN

How about this for a biography? In 1830 he was shipwrecked, 1831 married, 1832 wife dead, 1833 re-married and converted to Roman Catholicism, 1844 second wife died, 1849 married again, 1851 had a mental breakdown, 1852 died aged forty.

That was the life of the architect Augustus Welby Northmore Pugin. That's quite a name and some of his work was on the grand scale too for this is the man employed to design all that vertical detailing on the Houses of Parliament. He was responsible also for the rich interior. At the same time, his services were in demand in Surrey by Henry Drummond, Lord of the Manor of Albury.

Hidden away in the park is the old manor house which was originally Tudor and so that was the style adopted by Pugin when Drummond commissioned him to remodel the house. The alterations were drastic and the result is rather drastic too, but this isn't surprising, considering Pugin's emotional upheavals at this end of his life. He did give Albury Park House one very distinctive feature and that is the set of chimneys. There are sixty-three, all modelled on Tudor originals and all different. They can be glimpsed from the churchyard.

Also at Albury is a little snatch
of his interior design skills, then
being developed at Westminster. It is
the mortuary chapel designed by Henry
Drummond and to be found in the south
transept of the old church in the park
(access is permitted). The richly
decorated surfaces were inspired by
his enthusiasm for such schemes in
medieval Roman Catholic churches. Due
regard is paid to Protestantism
though, with the medieval image niche
in the transept being provided with a
Crucifixion scene rather than a statue
of the Blessed Virgin Mary, "from whom
no help can be derived," said
Drummond.

This work was carried out by
T.Early in red, blue and gold and is
enhanced further on sunny days by the
coloured light from the stained glass
windows which were provided by another
pioneer, W.Wailes of Newcastle. While
all this was going on Henry Drummond
was continuing a long battle, begun by
previous owners, to exclude people
from the Park.

Originally, the medieval village
was grouped around the church right
next to the manor house but by the
time Drummond bought the estate in
1819 all had been swept away. A new
village had been created beyond the
Park - the present day Albury. The
villagers still came into the Park to
use the church though. Drummond built
them a new one, right away at the
other end of the village. He foresaw
it being built of stone but returned
from a trip abroad to find it had been
built of brick which was a rare item
in Surrey at that time, (services
began in 1842). Then, overcoming
local opposition, Drummond had
services discontinued in the old
church. Pugin's work, however,
continued through all this and was
completed in 1844. This gave Drummond
what he wanted - his own chapel, in
the old manorial tradition, in what
was practically his own church.

Despite the displeasure this caused
he did make positive contributions to
the village. Hence today unsuspecting
motorists driving into The Street are
surprised by great Tudor chimneys
soaring out of the cottage roofs as
Pugin planned.

(13.3.87)

DRAMA AT WEYBRIDGE

Poor John Selwyn. I wonder what would have happened to him if his most famous exploit had gone wrong. He was the Keeper of the Royal Park of Oatlands at Weybridge which must have left him at peace in the countryside for much of the time. The court circle was a dangerous place though and every now and again the monarch would visit the Park in full expectation that Selwyn would have everything organised including a guarantee of hunting success.

To this end he and his men would drive suitable deer, including a noble stag of course, into a particular corner of the Park where he could later lead the hunting party. It was much more organised than that though. His men would be placed strategically, out of sight, to divert their fleeing quarry along a prescribed route - right in front of the hunting party. Success was vital. The monarch could not be allowed to look a failure, especially as this particular monarch was Elizabeth I. Being a woman did not keep her from the chase.

"I know I have the body of a weak and feeble woman but I have the heart and stomach of a king and a king of England too," she reassured her subjects, in her famous Armada speech. At the chase she was always there, in the front row. That was unfortunate on the day that John Selwyn realised to his horror that the fleeing stag was not going to bound along the intended route in front of Her Majesty. Instead, it appeared to be charging directly at her.

Quick as a flash he leapt upon its back, drew his knife and stabbed the beast through the throat. He brought it crashing down at Her Majesty's feet. Bravo Selwyn! His day ended in triumph rather than disaster.

In due course this momentous event was portrayed on his memorial brass in the parish church of Walton on Thames. The brass is particularly interesting because it is a palimpsest. In other words it has been worked on both sides. Normally such brasses have been turned over and worked at a later date but in this case both sides relate to Selwyn. The back is only lightly engraved, as though sketched out for approval, which it didn't get. The final version has various design changes.

Weybridge from Coxes Lock silo before its demolition.

I must confess I find it hard to
believe that Selwyn could leap on to
the back of a stag at full speed but
nevertheless something grand must have
happened. It had been a grand reign;
on this date in 1603, after forty four
years it was ending. Elizabeth,
defiant to the end, died on March 24.

(23.3.90)

KING JAMES AND HIS LOYAL SUBJECTS

On this day in 1603 began a new reign with the accession of James I. He was a keen sportsman and found good hunting in the local royal parks: Henley, Woking, Oatlands, Bagshot. Then there was the Bishop of Winchester's Castle and Park at Farnham which the new king visited so often that Bishop Bilson decided to lease it all out to him. Additionally there were the local estates of the King's loyal subjects and a quick tour round local churches will introduce many.

At Witley there is the memorial to Henry Bell of Rake House, Milford, and Lord of the Manor from 1615, who served as Clerk Comptroller of the Royal Household. Also at Witley lived Anthony Smith, Clerk of the Spicery. At Cranleigh is remembered Richard Cholmley, the King's Cupbearer.

At Weybridge Sir John Trevor, appointed Keeper of Oatlands Park nearby, where the new king came with his queen, Anne of Denmark, and their son, prior to the coronation.

He granted her the house and park in 1611. She was also the last royal owner of neighbouring Byfleet Manor. Through her, Denmark House in Chertsey may have got its otherwise unexplained name. The Chertsey Abbey lands were granted to Dr John Hammond, the King's physician.

Among the court favourites was Philip Hubert, Earl of Montgomery, who was such a whiz-kid he matriculated from New College, Oxford at the age of nine. He was granted the Royal Park of Henley. The chief Surrey favourite however, was Lord Edward Zouch, Marshall of the Household and, after 1620, Lord of the Manor of Woking. Here he entertained his king most lavishly on several occasions. The king spent much too, so that on one occasion he had to pawn £20,000 worth of jewels to pay for the royal progress - or so the story goes. It was while at Woking that the rumour broke that the king was dead. Quickly James despatched himself to London to show himself safe and sound - or as sound as could be expected of "the wisest fool in Christendom."

Among those knighted were Nicholas Lusher of Shoelands, Puttenham, at the coronation. At Stoke-next-Guildford two members of the Stoughton family have memorials; Sir Laurence knighted at Bagshot in 1611 and Sir George knighted at Oatlands in 1616. The Lord of the Manor of Wanborough was knighted at home when a royal progress paused there for refreshment. They were travelling from Loseley and that's the best starting place for a Jacobean tour.

There in the Great Hall hang the full-length portraits of the King and Queen, presented to commemorate one of their visits. Step into the Drawing Room and we see just how it was redecorated for such an occasion. Pad upstairs to the King's Bedroom to see the carpet specially commissioned still displaying proudly the thistle emblem of James's other kingdom of Scotland.

One of the most prominent reminders of the time is the Royal Arms displayed, since last century, over the main entrance to Abbot's Hospital in Guildford High Street, while its Royal Charter is displayed inside.

There isn't room for more but there is more for the seeking.

(24.3.89)

KING JOHN SPENT EASTER
AT WAVERLEY

So, it's Easter again and the need for a timely tale. Let's go over to the ruins of Waverley Abbey, near Farnham, where a tale will take us back to the year 1208. At that time the abbey had been in existence for 80 years and from its humble start was beginning to mature. The primitive shelters that had once sufficed were now being rebuilt into a more permanent and costly design. The expense was being borne by one of the priests, known as William of Broadwater.

Work had been in progress for three or four years, but it was always a slow business often hampered in those days by the effects of famine following bad harvests. Added to these problems, the wet years caused the River Wey to flood through this riverbank site. Nevertheless William persevered, only to have his efforts confounded by measures he couldn't have forseen. The King of England upset the Pope. As it was King John that is unlikely to surprise us, as the Victorians made an excellent job of blackening his name, seemingly for ever. He doesn't deserve his reputation, but on this occasion his dispute with the Pope did result in "interdict" - the Pope forbade access to church services and functions and privileges. Thus souls could not be saved from purgatory and fear usually brought the recalcitrant to heel.

Waverley
Abbey.

John did not come to heel. He
seized church property instead and
thus the rector of Broadwater found
his assets confiscated. Even worse,
for Waverley, that was where King John
chose to spend Easter week.
Presumably he intended to ignore the
Pope's ban and attend services and
evidently the brothers were also
expected to ignore the ban and provide
hospitality. We're left today
suspecting that he was not their most
welcome guest! No doubt some wished
he would travel on to his royal castle
at Guildford, or land himself on the
Bishop of Winchester at Farnham
Castle. Nevertheless, we've always
found virtue in making the best of a
bad job and so it must have been that
Easter. Somebody, somehow, worked
wonders on John for when he left he
directed that his seizure of William's
assets should cease, that William's
possessions should be returned to him
and, most importantly for Waverley,
his rents and other revenues should
once again be paid to him. Building
work could thus continue; Waverley
would continue to grow. I would
dearly love to know how the brothers
achieved that!

(27.3.86)

31

COMPTON'S SYMBOLIC CHAPEL

It was very early on a beautiful autumn morning back in 1983 that I drove down to Compton to draw the Watts Chapel. Fortunately the sun was still low and cast strong shadows between the relief work of the chapel walls where the lit bricks glowed a rich terracotta in their dewy dampness. Soon I was totally absorbed by the intricacies of the patterned surfaces. Back and forth I kept walking for closer looks to try and understand what I was trying to draw. In the end I settled for recording an impression. Go and see for yourselves and you'll soon see why!

It's the burial place of the Victorian artist G.F.Watts and was designed by his widow in 1896. It is all symbolic and quite a puzzle to unravel. The plan is a Circle of Eternity through which runs a Greek Cross of Faith - thus the walls between the cross arms are curved. Then the surfaces, inside and out, are richly decorated and here the puzzle begins, especially on the outside.

The designs are a weird sort of Art Nouveau with much Celtic influence, but the slightly later inside is a purer Art Nouveau . The terracotta panels were all made from local clay by local people. Seventy three workers are listed of whom four are credited with working on it every day for nearly two years. They certainly produced an astonshing piece of architecture although the inside gives me the creeps.

Now I understand it a little better since being lent recently a copy of "The Word in the Pattern" by Mrs G.F.Watts in which she explains her design. Thus the three orders of the archway are not to be read separately but as wedges with each being an angel, head lowest. Those that look down do so in sympathy while those that look up do so in hope. The second order is their winged bodies with their feathers marked with the peacock eye of watchfulness. All these are woven together with the Celtic Cord of Unity that is knotted in the third order. Each knot makes a cross, for Christianity, over the four corners of the Earth.

The capitals supporting the arches bear a standard architectural motif but used here in the belief that it was originally a feather - the breast feather of the comforting Mother bird. The columns below include the "I Am" with the alpha and omega.

The decorated surfaces into which all this is set represents an embroidered hanging or veil and is called The Garment of Praise. This isn't easy to follow, even with the book, but at least the angels along the top are clear - they are the praising angels with their musical instruments. Below them are more trumpets and a chequered pattern to represent night and day. Below that, against the arch, is the Phoenix rising from the flames. Further down are three weird upright objects, described as oil jars shaped as tear bottles, for the consecration of mourning, for healing wounds and for light in darkness. So it goes on.

(27.3.87)

LEFT
Roundheads at Farnham Castle;
one of the very few creative
images used in 'Seen in Surrey'.

BOTTOM RIGHT
Medieval stained glass figure
of St.Paul at Buckland Church.

BOTTOM LEFT
Head of John Touchet from his
memorial brass in Shere Church.

34

SEEKING BISHOP JOHN

Harebells

In East Horsley's parish church can be found a memorial to a Bishop of Exeter, who died in the village on this day, April 5th in 1478. Why we might ask, was a Bishop of Exeter in East Horsley?

The answer is that it was one of the manors belonging to Exeter and the bishops would visit from time to time, no doubt finding it convenient for visiting London. The land was already owned by Exeter back in the year of the Doomsday Book (1086), when Bishop Osbern and the King shared large parts of the Woking district and the King granted concessions to the Church. Thus the bishops had a customary right to use the King's woodland, valued as pasture for 120 pigs, and not pay anything.

Also at East Horsley were lands held by the archbishops of Canterbury and again had been so since before the days of the Doomsday Book. Therein we are told that the profits were used for clothing the monks at Canterbury.

Thus a visit from Bishop John Bowthe would not have surprised the villagers although, as far as we know, he was not expected to die. The memorial in the church is a brass of some rarity.. It is the only brass in Surrey to show an ecclesiastic kneeling at prayer and indeed in the whole country there is only one other. That's to Bishop Mayo in Hereford Cathedral but is a modern restoration.

Bishop Bowthe is shown fully robed in his vestments as for taking Mass. He should be wearing gloves but these have been left off, as has his tunic which would otherwise cover his vestments. All this can be recognised from other sources but the second reason for this brass being such a rarity is that the image is in profile and therefore very valuable for showing how the vestments were designed at the sides and for clues given as to what happens round the back.

Little is known about the man except that he was reputed to be a good administrator. He is thought to be the son of Sir Robert Bowthe of Dunham in Cheshire and that his mother was Douce, the daughter and co-heir of Sir Richard Venables of nearby Bollin. John would therefore have been of good birth and may illustrate the familiar story that younger sons were put to the Church as there were no estates for them; John would have been the third son.

Whatever his beginnings he certainly did well. In 1457 he comes into the records when appointed Treasurer of York. Two years later he became Archdeacon of Richmond and the next year, Warden of the Collegiatae Church of Manchester. Then, in 1465, he was consecrated Bishop of Exeter.

(5.4.91)

35

ABINGER'S CRUCIFIXION

Lent Lilies

Abinger, up on Leith Hill, always makes a good destination for a trip in the country. The way up to it is long and steep, by lanes cut deep into the sandstone and enclosed with boughs. Summer makes the way green and mysterious, golding in autumn to a thrill of wind and just as beautiful when bare twigs pattern the frosty blue overhead. Now it's greening up again and a little sunshine brings a warm smell out of the leafy woods; so different from last autumn's scent of decay.

As the moon goes through its cycles so Easter makes its annual shift among the seasons. Villagers once watched it carefully and many still insist that the success of their vegetables results from the seeds having been planted on Good Friday. The truth probably has more to do with it being a holiday and providing opportunity. [I have been told since that Good Friday was essential because while Christ's body lay upon the soil even the forces of evil were dormant and gave the seeds a chance.]

There was also at this time the chance to join in with special Easter festivities. Up in the Midlands, in the Middle Ages, wagons rolled through the streets as mobile stages upon which the people acted out the Easter story. Certain workers at Nottingham were inspired to record what they saw, upon the alabaster panels which they carved for the rest of the year. Such panels were very popular and travelled widely once sold. Three are now displayed in Abinger church, presented by Sir Edward Beddington-Behrens.

Like the rest of the panels they are only small but no less beautiful for that. One offers the severed head of John the Baptist - always a popular subject because it was easily recognisable and fitted well the small panel. It's probably a bit gory for some people's taste today but must have been more poignant 500 years ago when execution was a real threat to the unwary; the lord of many a Surrey manor ended his days on the block.

The Crucifixion scene is another Abinger subject and what a scene it is too. So much is depicted in so small an area that it's a marvel of design, remaining balanced and clear. It's also mighty difficult to sketch! The tight design leaves no room for error in judging the proportions. Drawing makes you really look at it. The pen finds the two thieves on their crosses, tucked into the background, and a nice Roman soldier asserting his indifference with downcast eyes, and so on. It's all rather weathered now but still shows so clearly because such a sure hand carved it in the first place.

The craftsman chipped away carefully at the under-cutting to throw as much as possible into high relief. Then the flickering candlelight would do the rest, filling the hollows with dark shadows and catching the upper surfaces to make their painted details glow in reds and golds. Rembrandt would have loved it.

Today, April 7th, is the date most probable for the actual Crucifixion of Jesus, according to those who research such things.

(7.4.89)

COBHAM MILL
as it was before the
Cobham Mill Preservation Trust
undertook its restoration.
Now the wheel is back in
place on the left side of
the building, from this
viewpoint, and all the
surrounds have been enhanced.

38

SAVING COBHAM MILL

No doubt many of you have recognised the watermill, as it is right beside the road from Cobham to Leatherhead. Those who have been passing for several years will have watched it falling into greater and greater decay but now it is good news. The mill has been going through a complete restoration.

The earliest record of a mill in Cobham is in the Doomsday Book (1086) but the exact site is not known. The present mill site was recorded as such in 1534 when Richard Sutton leased it from the landowner Chertsey Abbey.

The building we see today dates from 1822 and shows the simplest way of harnessing the power of a river; by putting the wheel into the natural fall of the water but in a side channel to avoid the worst damage by floods. This spot is particularly prone to flooding.

Until 1953 there were two mills here, working side by side, until the need for road widening demanded the destruction of the second and much larger one. For some time it had worked as a steam mill but both mills stopped working in the 1920's. The restorers think 1928 was the last year corn was ground here.

The smaller mill was due for demolition too but suggestions in the press that it would make a fine focal point for a riverside park prompted its retention. It has taken a long time to come about but once the mill is restored there are plans to enhance the site around it.

In the intervening years the National Rivers Authority was established and found itself the new owner of the mill. As it needed to restore the riverside, to fulfil its own regulations, it leased the mill to a group of local people who founded the Cobham Mill Preservation Trust and began fund raising. The response was sufficient to fund a monthly working party and with the expert knowledge of local volunteer engineers all the major work was completed in six months. Inside, all the machinery was put back into place to show visitors how an undershot watermill worked although there are no plans to grind corn again.

Of the smaller details, one of the last but significant tasks was putting the wooden paddles back into the wheel to have it turning by the summer. Then, when the island has been landscaped, visitors can enjoy the industrial archaeology, sit and have a cup of tea, gently watch the River Mole ease by and know that a good job has been done.

(19.4.91)

PLANTS TELLING

EASTER STORY

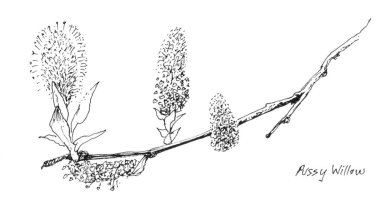

Pussy Willow

On Palm Sunday no doubt many of our churches continued the tradition of using Pussy Willow to symbolise the palm branches of the Easter story. Strewing the floor with Marsh Marigolds seems to have died out. Sadly the country names and folklore of our plants are dying from lack of usage. Once the Easter story could be told with ease to a grandchild by a Surrey cottager in his garden.

He wouldn't have had the Olive from the Garden of Gethsemane. He wouldn't have a Judas Tree (although introduced in 1596) but he could point to the Elder tree over the pig pen and tell how Judas hanged himself upon such a tree. He'd explain how it was now lowly and twisted with repentance. Granny might disagree and say that the tree provided the timber for the Cross. Still it bows its head.

The Speedwell in the lawn was named after Veronica who wiped the face of Jesus with her handkerchief as He staggered with his Cross to Calvary. The Hemp Agrimony in the hedgerow provided the fibre for the rope that bound Jesus to the Cross to prevent his weight pulling him free of the nails. The blood fell as Holly (Holy) berries on the plant sacred to Jesus for it sprang from his footprints on Earth.

Those Passion wounds are remembered by the five little petals of the Avens (Geum). When he died the Pasque Flower (Pulsatilla vulgaris) closed its flowers and hung its head. The Virgin Mary cried, her tears falling as Lilies-of the Valley. Other tears fell upon the leaves of the Lungwort (Pulmonaria), gleaming as the white spots. Above them the flower heads bear blooms of two colours, blue for the Virgin's robe and red for her tear-raw eyes. Her holy plant, the Cowslip, yielded herbal remedies for distressed faces. Granny might argue that the red is from the blood spots upon the blue robe.

Man has always wondered which plant made the Crown of Thorns. In church the Blackthorn or Hawthorn was used in this country. A species of Euphorbia (Spurge) is often claimed to be the likeliest contender but in 1597 to this country came another contender from the Holy Land, Christ's Thorn, Paliuris spina-Christi. However these last three plants are not likely to have been in a Surrey cottage garden.

Later in the year the Passion Plant tells the story. The crown is the ring of coloured bracts. Inside, the stamens are like nails and the stigmas like hammers. There are only ten petals to represent the Disciples so these are the faithful. Hiding behind the flower can be seen a symbol for St Peter, making eleven. Judas, the twelfth, was of course hanging from the elder Tree.

The Ox-eye Daisy is the Holy Plant of Mary Magdalene who discovered the resurrection. Then the Pasque Flower lifted its head once again and opened its blooms to show the halo of stamens glowing with the promise of eternal life. All the other flowers had deserted Calvary. Then as the Virgin cried with joy and her tears can still be seen as the sparkling raindrops on her scalloped and folded shawl (Our Lady's Mantle, Alchemilla mollis).

The whole story can be told in one of our favourite flowers, the Lent Lily or Daffodil. There are six petals for the lenten Sundays, with the main top petal being for Palm Sunday. The stamens and stigmas are the symbols of the the Passion and the trumpet heralds the Resurrection. It seems a shame to silence such stories into print, so tell a little folklore this Easter.   (19.4.84)

40

EASTER FLOWERS

Daffodil
Cowslip
Pasque Flower
Lungwort

GODALMING'S FLAMBARD

Godalming Church. 1982.

Perhaps this was only malicious gossip recorded by Florence of Worcester but on the other hand none of the other chroniclers had a good word for Ranulph. He was universally disliked. His king wasn't exactly popular either. He was particularly feared in Surrey in case he increased the areas covered by Forest Law as opposed to Common Law. That would mean that the law was basically the king's will. It was highly restrictive and repressive and savage in its penalties, giving the king a total power enjoyed by no other king in Europe. All revenues went directly to the king and with Ranulph's avaricious mind in control, coupled with his knowledge of Surrey, the people of Surrey were worried.

The king did indeed extend Forest Laws in the county, beginning with his own manors at Brookwood, Guildford, Woking and parts of Stoke. Ralph, for his part, was corrupting Common Law, sending his agents out into the Shire Courts to increase the fines. Then Ralph couldn't bear to see damages being awarded and so those too got milked off.

"Oh he'd do anything for his boss, he would," claimed a loud voice as we jostled along Church Street in Godalming. It was an appropriate snatch of conversation to overhear, for Godalming Church once had a vicar who earned his boss £10,000. That was Ranulph, known as Flambard (burning torch) because of the anger he fired with his trouble-making. His boss was not so much the bishop as the king, William II, because Ranulph was his chaplain, rose to be his right hand man and acted as regent whenever William was out of the country.

It was Ranulph who came up with the lucrative ploy of pretending to invade Normandy. The English fighting force duly assembled at the coast, 20,000 of them, with their ten shillings travelling expenses. Ranulph's agents went among them collecting it - not for shipment but for the royal coffers - and then the soldiers were all sent home!

Part of the hatred towards Ranulph was no doubt due to his having been born of low rank. William II and his brother Henry I were ahead of their time in promoting able administrators whatever their social background. These legal and fiscal whizz kids created a permanent civil service that had no equal in Europe.

William used Ranulph in other ways, like making him Bishop of Durham to spite the Archbishop of Canterbury - not bad going for an ex-clerk of Chancery. Durham was the richest see but not for long. The next king had to take it under his protection "on account of the injuries and violence which Ralph the bishop did to them in his lifetime." That lifetime ended in 1128. Parts of his church at Godalming survive in the present structure while the £ s.d. system of counting money which he devised survived till 1971. He also has the dubious privilege of having been the first prisoner in the Tower of London, and the first prisoner to escape! (10.5.85)

MILESTONES

A milestone is such a familiar expression that it is easy to overlook the real thing along Surrey roadsides. They are not without interest - who set them up, paid for them, cared for them, and how many different types are there? Few people in Surrey know all the answers and so at present they are being sought out and recorded.

The total has reached 135 so far with previously unknown ones coming to light. In a county with little good stone many have been carted off to serve other purposes. One was even offered to an antiques dealer.

The one illustrated can be found in Egham at the end of the High Street where it turns off to Staines. The style of lettering gives an 18th century date but we cannot see whether there is a precise date carved into the back as it is embedded in a wall. So far the oldest dated stone located in Surrey is of 1741.

Egham High Street may seem an odd place to find one but this was once a thriving coaching village on the approach to Staines Bridge. Over this came one of the more important roads to the West County, so that it was reported that eighty coaches a day went through Egham at the height of their fashion.

Today, only the Red Lion survives out of the coaching inns. It displays a 16th century date but most of what we see is typical Surrey refacing in later brick and tile. Its hardly noticeable in a street of such varied architecture. Also easily overlooked is another reminder of the coaching days, down in the small public garden nearly opposite Strode's College. It's an early 19th century water pump and quite massive compared with the usual garden pumps. That's because it had a more important purpose than supplying domestic needs. This one was to make the water carrier's job easier when it was up on the coach road approaching Staines Bridge. There hundreds of gallons of water were needed to lay the choking dust cast up by all the coaches. After all, it would never do for society ladies to arrive all whitened with dust, now would it!

18 Miles from Hyde Park Corner

REMEMBERING FRANCIS

To the north of Guildford there is still beautiful countryside to enjoy, due in part to the land still belonging to the Sutton Place estates. These were created by Henry VIII, out of the royal lands of Woking, to reward the Weston family for their services. Theirs is a family with some interesting members, apart from the Sir Richard who founded the Wey Navigation. There was Francis, for example, who was what today's slang would call a "whizz kid".

At the age of 15, in 1526, he went off to serve in Henry VIII's court as a page and was soon a favourite of both the king and later his queen, Anne Boleyn. He was such a favourite that he partnered the king at sport, at a time when Henry was reckoned to be the finest athlete in Europe. In particular, he was counted the supreme champion at tennis. Of course, most opponents were wary of beating the all-powerful egotist but not Francis Weston. He played for money, beat the king and raked in the winnings, not once but again and again. The royal accounts show that Henry did pay up too, but we don't know whether Francis was such a favourite that the king let him win. He certainly liked him enough to pay out for a wedding present when Francis married the rich Anne Pickering in 1530.

Then there was dice - more a matter of luck than skill but Francis was lucky and kept winning at that too, the wager was £46 on one occasion so we're not talking fun money; it was more than his annual salary. Another game, called "Imperial", which is thought to have been a card game, brought him more winnings. He was not only a reckless gambler but was shooting up through the ranks as promotion followed promotion. He obviously felt very confident about his position in the king's affections.

It was the same with the new queen. He was made Knight of the Bath in order to escort her to the wedding ceremony because nobody else would do it. Later he was made Gentleman of her Privy Chamber. Some thought he was not the perfect gentleman. Just because the Queen knew she was coarse and loved flattery, it was not for Francis to provide it quite so lavishly. This was to prove to be his downfall.

There were those at court who resented his success, including several of Surrey's great landowners, and so when the storm broke over Anne Boleyn's supposed infidelity it was upon Francis that eyes turned.

On April 24th 1536 the secret inquiry was initiated and arrests followed quickly, of the queen herself and of her immediate circle. That included Sir Francis Weston. He was at the peak of his career, happily married, proud father of a baby son and apparently unconcerned that his gambling debts amounted to nearly ten times his annual salary.

He was told to prepare for execution on 16th May. His mother and his wife bid 100,000 crowns for his life but to no avail. Thus at the Tower of London on this day, 17th May, Sir Francis Weston, aged 25, was executed for adultery with the Queen of England.   (17.5.91)

GUILDFORD'S RIVERSIDE

The illustration will be familiar to many readers. It's the Town Mill beside the Yvonne Arnaud Theatre viewed from Millmead. Although Guildford has seen many changes in the last few years, this view has not been one of them. The building is one of the few substantial watermills along the River Wey: a fine brick structure dating from 1770, although there have been mills here for perhaps a thousand years.

Most people think of watermills grinding corn to produce flour but Surrey mills have served many industries, from cloth and paper making to grinding wood for dyes. This one, however, was indeed a corn mill, until 1894. In its last phase it worked towards charitable ends, with the profits donated to the poor of Guildford. Far more people benefitted after 1896 when Guildford Corporation converted it to pumping water round the Borough. Today, as far as I know, it is used by the Yvonne Arnaud Theatre.

It was while I was looking at the Theatre and thinking how well it had stood the test of time when so many early 60's buildings were now looking thoroughly decrepit, that the inevitable local mine of information arrived at my shoulder.

Did I know, he enquired, that the theatre site was an iron foundry till 1942? Well, despite the criticisms of the theatre when it was built, it must surely be better-looking than an iron foundry, especially when Guildford has failed so dismally to make its riverside a major feature of the town.

Oh yes, he went on, it did very well in Victorian times, when Filmer and Mason had it. My ears pricked up. Filmer and Mason rang a bell. Only the week before I'd been noting cast iron grave markers in Cranleigh churchyard and they were made in Guildford by that company.

Such grave markers are scattered through Surrey churchyards and not much notice is taken of them, which is a shame. They're gradually rusting away and likely to disappear. Although they were cheaper than stone memorials they must, nevertheless, have been quite expensive as each had to be a one-off casting.

A different sort of memorial was then pointed out - a plaque in the grass outside the extension to St. Nicolas's Church, to a man who fell and broke his arm and died there. That was a former incumbent, Dr John Monsell, who was a well-known hymn writer. He transferred to Guildford from Egham and they story they tell there is that he fell out of the roof while telling workmen how to repair it. In truth there was no roof at all, as the church at that time was being rebuilt. Monsell apparently fell over the foundation and sustained the injury that led to complications from which he died. The new church was opened in 1876.   (19.5.89)

46

Guildford: Town Mill 1770+
G. Hawkins 1982/3.

MINT STREET

C. Hawkins 85/88

OLD GODALMING

I celebrated the sunshine after rain recently with a walk around one of the older corners of Godalming. Finding a parking space in Station Road, I went off to view the station again - back in the sixties I'd used it every day and the rise through the trees to the forecourt seems just the same today.

The main building was softly gold in the spring sunshine, looking clean and spruce, making it the most attractive station scene in any Surrey town. It opened for service in 1859, as did Haslemere which also retains its main building but the station approach there is quite hideous.

The early date means the buildings have a domestic appearance. The railway companies had not yet developed the 'institutional' style that makes later stations so immediately recognisable. Ordinary everyday materials were used instead of the mass produced components that we think of as 'railway architecture'. Those were in use by 1868 when Leatherhead station was built. That too is a fine example of its style [as is Caterham which has since been redecorated - Ed]. From ten years earlier is the station at Farnham, built like a five-bay town house and looking somehow stark.

Godalming's station is not the original. That was built towards Farncombe in 1849 because it was the end of the line. Only when the engineers pressed on towards Portsmouth was it possible to build a new one closer to the town. In fact it is right next to the old medieval town and so I set off down Mill Lane to wander through the narrow streets that still record those days.

Despite all the alterations there are still plenty of reminders of earlier times, from the black and white timber-framed houses that still survive (more than in any other Surrey town), to the Old Granary opposite the Corn Mill; that was my next stopping place as I had been told that at some time the waterwheel had been replaced by a turbine that was visible from the road. Sure enough there was the great pipe by the mill carrying water from the River Ock. Cast into it was all the information I wanted - "Gilbert Gilkes and Gordon Ltd. Kendal, 1940".

Leaning over the bridge, looking at the mill and watching the river flow down through the water plants was a very pleasing way to while away a few moments. The bridge parapet includes bricks with a decorative indented motif. I don't remember seeing any others from the same mould; can other examples still be seen?

Moving up the hill I went looking for houses connected with Godalming's ancient cloth trade. No 22 Mint St., has recently been investigated so I went to remind myself which one it was. It's not difficult to find and there, sure enough, were the upper windows raised up through the eaves to give extra light.   (20.5.88)

Great Fosters, Egham.
C. Hawkins 1982 ©

The illustration of Great Fosters, Egham, used
for publicising the newly formed Surrey Gardens
Trust, which was launched from here. The hotel
has an historic garden of importance.

NAUGHTY VICAR - NICHOLAS ANDREWES

Any vicar who impersonated his parishioners from the pulpit on Sundays would catch my attention, especially if he did it so well that they recognised themselves and complained. Such a cleric was Nicholas Andrewes at Godalming and St Nicolas at Guildford.

He was a victim of his own Puritan times. The Long Parliament invited parishes to notify it of any "scandalous ministers" who were hindering the new reforms and at this time Nicholas Andrewes upset some of his Godalming parishioners. Probably they were the vociferous minority, but, nevertheless, they made the vicar the subject of a complaint to Parliament and went to considerable lengths to blacken his name. In particular, they denounced him for having Roman Catholic leanings.

In reality, it was the complainants who were most in the wrong. They were clinging to the old religion, complaining that Andrewes was changing the traditional services and arrangements in the church whereas that was just what Parliament had ordered him to do. He got on with pushing ahead with reforms, as we'd expect of someone recorded elsewhere as a great Protestant. We can imagine him disregarding a few old diehards, hence the complaint that he was "very proud, presumptuous, imperious and tyrannical."

They snatched at anything they could interpret as being "popish," like having a crucifix in his bed chamber, (how did they know?) and "Romish pictures which he keepeth secretly behind the hangings in his said house." How did they know that too? Most likely these had been removed from church, as ordered, but it must have been very difficult for him to burn something he had been brought up to regard as sacred. Perhaps he hid them for safe keeping in what were very changeable times; Queen Mary had already tried to destroy Protestantism once, so what else might happen?

The Parliamentary Committee of Religion was swamped with complaints. They didn't check them, they heard no witnesses for the prosecution and certainly none for any defence.

Indeed they viewed such actions as indefensible and so a complaint secured conviction. Numerous clerics were deprived of their livings.

Nicholas Andrewes was no exception. He was imprisoned, on land and aboard ship, to hasten the end of his life, as they put it . It was a sad end for someone who couldn't please everyone. No wonder that they found he'd nipped off down the pub and joined in with gambling or that he and the Parson of Compton would go off to Southampton "to make merry together". It was there that they complained that he drank to the health of the Pope! Presumably that gesture was one of satire. After all, Andrewes seems to have enjoyed a touch of satire, if we are to believe that he did impersonations of his parishioners from the pulpit! (2.6.89)

C Hawkins 1986

CHURCH THAT SHRANK

Many of you will have driven past the small church at Little Bookham and not realised it was there. It's worth seeing, if only for what is missing.

Church after church reveal how they have grown over the centuries, but this one has shrunk. The fact is apparent immediately, even from the outside, for still embedded in the south wall is the evidence of a lost south aisle. There you'll find a series of capitals still linked by an arcade of round arches from the 12th Century. It was removed before the middle of the 15th century but exactly why or when is unknown. Presumably the village had shrunk and the extra accommodation wasn't needed or perhaps there wasn't enough money to repair or support it. This royal manor has a very tangled history of lordship.

Tradition has it that the aisle was burnt down in the 13th Century. Certainly in 1933 the charred remains of a gnomon was found in the centre of a sundial. It was a medieval sundial known as a scratch dial and would have been on the south wall to catch the sun. The scratches radiating across its face marked the times of services. These vary from dial to dial, but Little Bookham's like most others, has a line for nine and 12 o'clock. Those were the times for Mass. Hence their other name of Mass dials.

When the south wall was altered the block of stone was too valuable to discard and was incorporated into a window splay (second from east in nave; top left hand angle). Fortunately the dial was left facing outwards to be rediscovered all these hundreds of years later.

What has not been discovered is the patron saint to whom this church would have been dedicated. This year [1986] being its 900th anniversary, the celebrations include a festal evensong during which this lovely little church will be dedicated to All Saints. The preacher will be the Bishop of Guildford.

Inside, you'll be able to see the round arches even more architecturally. The capitals are unweathered, catching the light across their scalloped surfaces. Below each the abacus stone was chamfered off to lighten appearances, but the chamfer is hollow to catch the shadows and increase the sense of depth in times when the interior was far less well lit than today.

Here it is easier to bridge the gap back to those Domesday times when the Hansard family probably built this church as their memorial chapel. You'll find it up a drive westwards of the bend in Manor House Lane, that links Lower Road with the main Guildford/Leatherhead Road. (6.6.86)

THE BLACK PRINCE

On this day, June 8, Edward the Black Prince, died. If you have walked from Wisley, down over the river and up by Byfleet Manor, you have followed a route he knew well.

Records show he took a keen interest in this royal manor, visiting many times and leaving his royal household there at others. He stabled his royal horses at Wisley, kept his brood mares and foals in the meadows, enquired about his fish and his swans, and thought his common was set alight to spite him. Twice he was Patron of Wisley Church and up at the manor he had new kitchens built. So who was he?

On June 15, 1330 Queen Philippa presented King Edward III, holder of Byfleet Manor, with a son and heir to the throne. He was named Edward too. Seven years later the Byfleet folk heard that their manor had been passed to the prince, together with other lands, to suit his new position, for the prince had received the earldom of Cornwall and had been promptly upgraded to duke. This was the first dukedom conferred by an English king. Today it is still the tradition that the eldest son of the monarch holds that title.

Edward went with his father to campaign in the Hundred Years War. Thus when he was 16, he distinguished himself at the Battle of Crecy and won his spurs. He continued to earn military fame. His greatest moments were commanding the famous Battle of Poitiers and capturing the French king, John II. This gave England great bargaining power at Bretigny. The resulting treaty brought a nine year respite and a ransom of £500,000 for their king, who was released after the first payment.

From that treaty King Edward gained sovereignty over Gascony. The next year he instituted Edward, the prince with the black armour, as governor. All this was good news for the Byfleet and Wisley folk. Most of them depended on his good fortune for their own.

The Black Prince stabled his horses at Wisley.

Four years later they heard that Edward was off to Spain to fight for Pedro, King of Castile. No doubt they heard about his great victory at Najera. Did they hear that his health failed and he had to return to Bordeaux? Did they hear of his troubles in Gascony and his leading a massacre at Limoges to combat rebellion against his misrule?

In 1371 they would certainly know that he resigned in favour of his brother, John of Gaunt, Duke of Lancaster, because he returned to England and to Byfleet. Loyal knights came with him. One was William de Seint Omer who became yeoman and park gamewarden. Parts of Wisley had been added to Byfleet Park and so the parson had to be compensated for loss of tithes. Soon these Wisley lands and mill were to be awarded to William de Seint Omer for his services in Gascony and especially Poitiers. Perhaps there is a twinge of conscience here for William had fallen from favour and only recently been pardoned.

In 1375 Edward was in Byfleet in July, August and September. Within a year he was dead. He was never king, for he was outlived by his father, but his son became Richard II. Much of their landscape remains; the manor house has been rebuilt but is till a splendid reminder that our quiet corners have great tales to tell.

(8.6.84)

FARNHAM EVENINGS

The drawing of a church tower, large enough for double bell-openings and tall corner pinnacles, will be recognised by many readers as that at Farnham. The pinnacles were added by Ewan Christian in 1865 and, to my way of thinking, add considerably to the visual statement made by the church in its landscape. Driving off the Hog's Back, they pop up over the treetops to encourage anyone to explore further. With time to spare, it's a call worth answering.

Downing Street and the Church Lanes remain much as they have been all my life and a few generations before. With other town centres having been modernised or ripped apart for road improvements, it's increasingly difficult to find such corners illustrating continuity.

A couple of highly rated Georgian houses stand at the bottom of Downing Street - Nos 3 and 4. The doorway of No 3 (built in 1717) is claimed to be one of the finest examples of cut brickwork in the country. The wish to see it again, before including it in a book, was what took me wandering the streets on an unexpectedly cold morning.

Better still is to visit on a sunny summer evening. Then the low sun brings out the glorious colour of the bricks. Only those from certain local clay pits have the rich orange tinge that makes them so special. Then, as the sun finally drops, the bottom of Castle Street purples into shadow while the upper part still shines brightly. It only lasts a few minutes but the pleasure lasts for years.

Totally different is the reward for tottering over the ironstone sets that cobble the narrow ways along Upper, Middle and Lower Church Lanes. They loop round the back of the upper part of Downing Street and bring you along the side of the great grassy space that is Farnham churchyard - a perfect setting for a medieval church.

Inside the Victorians have left it disappointing, but outside it's a grand building with a regular succession of attractive views. Again it's the soft evening light that can work wonders jiggling over the detailed surfaces of the Church Lane frontages offset by the grey masses of the church.

Much that you see is 19th century - the Victorians had a fine eye for the picturesque. Here they were given a good guide by the earlier cottages from some 300 years ago. Of particular interest is that some of the brickwork is not brick at all. Look very closely at Nos 1 and 2 in Lower Church Lane and you will find that the 'bricks' are, in fact, mathematical tiles bonded in their usual way to give the illusion of a smart, fashionable, Georgian facade. The date 1757 appears on one of the tiles.

Social pressure to keep up with the latest fashions must have been high in such a notably Georgian town as Farnham. Current pressures lead to much rebuilding of our town centres but the best of Farnham is still there to explore on a quiet sunny evening.

(16.6.89)

THE FRENCH TAKE GUILDFORD CASTLE

Guildford Castle Keep.
C. Howkins. 1986

THE FRENCH TAKE GUILDFORD CASTLE

The foreign soldiers spread into the little town of Guildford awaiting command from the advance party. Would the royal castle resist their invasion now that the king had fled towards Winchester, or would they have to take it by force or by seige? They already had Rochester, Bletchingley and Reigate Castles and soon, without battle, they'd take Guildford.

All was going well for the French, over here by invitation of the English barons in the aftermath of Magna Carta which King John had taken up arms. This was because his great ally, the Pope, had declared the document illegal.

The Pope's decision was based on four arguments. Primarily, that only the Pope could agree to such a document because he was the overlord of the barons, and had been since 1213 when King John had surrendered his lands to the Pope. Secondly, Magna Carta was not valid in law because the barons had been judges in their own case. Thirdly and fourthly, it was an insult fo the king and to the people of England.

That lot delighted King John but then he lost his great ally because the Pope went and died. The barons were in need of fresh support too, and so, in desperation, called upon the French Dauphin Louis, to help them defeat John and accept the crown of England for his trouble.

This seems odd for a nation who already resented foreign interference and who already liked things done according to the traditions and law of the land. This was all in Louis's favour, however, for he did have a legal claim to the English throne. This was through his wife, Blanche of Castile, who was the grand-daughter of a previous king, Henry II. Furthermore Louis claimed that it was John who lacked the legal entitlement to the throne because he had murdered the lawful heir, Arthur of Brittany. Additionally, he had been condemned for treason by Richard I.

This last claim had conveniently overlooked the fact that John had been pardoned. Words hadn't solved anything. Action was needed and the troops were on the move. The royalists were on the run. Resistance in the south-east was low because royalists like the Earl of Surrey joined the rebels in the better hope of safeguarding their lands and possessions. Thus the earl's castle at Reigate surrendered. The bishop's castle at Farnham did the same and Winchester gave no permanent shelter to John. As he fled, so London and the south-east fell to the French and English baronial alliance.

John then died. That seemed to leave the way clear for Louis. Momentum began foundering when the French and English began distrusting each other. Louis had to return to France to solve problems there and when he returned his cause was lost.

The Earl of Pembroke was acting as regent and negotiated peace. The French were given safe conduct out of the country and a nine year old boy, rightful heir to the throne, became King Henry III. He ruled for the next fifty-six years.   (19.6.87)

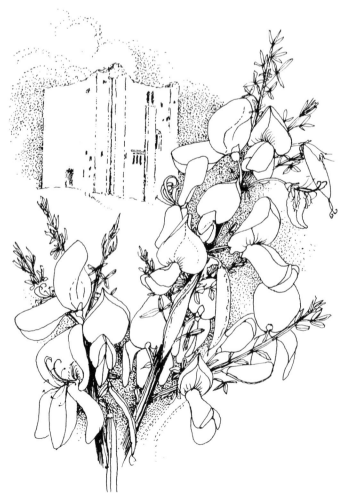

FLEE TO THE KING

On this day, July 1st, 1549 an alarming message was sent into Surrey: all noblemen and gentlemen were ordered to the safety of the king at Windsor Castle. The message was sent by the Council of Regency, acting for Edward VI who was still only twelve years old. The Council's task was to hold the country together after the long reign of the powerful Henry VIII. Now, eighteen months into the reign of a minor, the disaffected were getting restless.

Through June the Earl of Arundel, who was jointly Earl of Surrey and Sussex, became aware of this and sufficiently confident of its seriousness for him to inform a fellow member of the King's Council. Arundel was respected and his warning heeded and thus came the message. It must have caused some dismay in Guildford, to say the least. Most of the population had grown up in peace under Henry VIII; so much so that the County Gaol at Guildford Castle was ill maintained. There would be no secure stronghold there.

Henry VIII's troubles had not brought Surrey people into armed conflict so they'd never had to show where their loyalties lay. This posed a problem when it came to raising forces. Consequently, having received the Earl's letter of June 29th the Council directed on the 30th that their county officer, Sir Christopher More of Loseley, should raise troops he could trust and therefore to ignore the usual procedure of calling up the County Levies. The next day however came the order to flee.

Sir Christopher no doubt passed the responsibility to the Crown's Military commander, the Lord Lieutenant. That sounds a familiar title today but was then fairly new. Invented by Henry VIII, it was only given official recognition by the Council of Edward VI two years before these troubles, the office was held by a trusted royalist, Sir Anthony Browne.

Detail of Loseley.

Just to get us all confused, there were two Sir Anthony Brownes, father and son. This story concerns the son, the first Lord Montagu, his father having died a few months earlier, in 1548. This family was one of the great Surrey landowners and needed to be - as staunch Roman Catholics they were heavily and regularly fined for not attending Protestant services. Their loyalty to the Crown however, was not in question.

Browne and More and their team worked fast and well. Plans for the revolt were crushed. Those implicated and caught, were hanged. Surrey settled back to the old routines and the next year it was safe for the king to make a progress round his royal palaces in Surrey and in so doing took a long detour south to visit Guildford. (1.7.88)

C. Hawkins
9·6·84

TALES OF REBELLION

Beside the pub in the main street of Compton there's a footpath, lined with geraniums, that dips down into a hollow of broken shadows before curling away between Queen Anne's Lace and an excitement of insects. It climbs out of the valley, past the farm, out on the flanks of a broad green vale. The path heads for Hurtmore although it's the Hog's Back beyond the vale that commands attention, while lying among the trees below is Field Place.

During the evolution of this site it came into royal possession so that King Edward IV was able to grant it to a certain Sir Thomas St Leger. He moved in the highest circles, marrying Anne, the Duchess of Exeter, who had a brother called Richard. He, on this day, 6th July, in 1483 was crowned king of England as Richard III. He was a good soldier and a good organiser but not a good ruler of the English so in two years time he'd be fighting for his crown on Bosworth Field. Before that though, the disaffected, led by the Duke of Buckingham had already conspired against him.

The leader of the insurgents in Surrey was none other than Sir Thomas St Leger; being as ruthlessly ambitious as his brother-in-law. Sadly for him, it all went wrong. The Kent insurgents broke out before the planned day and thereby warned King Richard. The Duke of Buckingham was captured and executed at Salisbury. St Leger fled south west to the Duchy of Exeter but was hunted down, captured, and executed at Exeter.

He was also attainted, so his lands could not be passed on to his family and they reverted to the Crown. King Richard gave them to one of his more loyal servants, William Mistelbroke. His good fortune didn't last long either because the next king reversed the decisions in favour of St Leger's heiress, Anne.

It's a grand story to ponder up on the hillside, so close to the main road yet so quiet. At least it would have been had I not gone on Compton's fete day. The loudspeaker system was very effective and the races most exciting. It was not annoying, just very English. (6.7.84)

60

WHEELED RARITIES

Mr Henry Jackson has had a passion for collecting 'bygones' since he bought his wife a plough as a garden ornament. That was twenty years ago and now the collection is so large it's open to the public as the Old Kiln Museum at Tilford.

Each year it creeps a bit further over the ten acre site and last winter was no exception. Apart from improving some of the displays there was the major undertaking of providing a massive cart shed. It's to house a magnificent loan of vehicles from the stores of the Museum of English Rural Life at Reading. They have not been on view for 25 to 30 years, but arrived at Tilford in time for a public viewing last season. Now they're displayed under cover in a naturalistic way - lined up as in days of old.

So, following directions I looked down lines of wagons and carts in search of a rarity I had never seen before - a First World War horse ambulance. I didn't know what to expect and so paused eventually by a dark blue 'crate' on two wheels, simply because I couldn't imagine it was. This was indeed the ambulance, confirmed Mr Jackson with a warm smile under his thick white hair.

The museum's collection of wagons alone illustrates eight county styles. Now the theme has been extended further with the loan from Reading, including - a phaeton, a gig and a governess's cart, a Victoria and, of course, the ambulance.

It wasn't for rescuing injured soldiers, but injured horses - that's why it looks like a crate. The detachable shafts can be transferred from one end to the other for getting in and out of tight situations.

The ends themselves are double doors, divided in the middle to make four. The bottom pair can be repositioned to make a ramp for easy entry. The upper two can also be repositioned to make a side guard to guide the horse in. Should it be unable to stand it could be slung from an overhead metal loop. Cleverly, that is in fact the axle which loops usefully over the top of the vehicle rather than passing straight underneath it. Thus the body of the vehicle can be lowered close to the ground to make it easier to get the horse in.

It was all very carefully designed, but then so are all the old bygones. Mr Jackson slid his hand along some decorative chamfering on a nearby cart - "Not just beautiful," he murmured; "practical. Cuts away excess weight without losing strength."

(13.7.90)

ABOVE
Reigate Brewery before destruction
for redevelopment of town centre.

ABOVE RIGHT
Inside the last of Cobham's Bake
Houses before its destruction for
redevelopment.

BELOW
Example of Surrey barns, many of
which are threatened by neglect.

BUILDING RARITIES

It must have been very tantalising for a hungry rodent to be able to smell a whole banquet of corn and not be able to reach it. The outwitting farmer had learned the cunning of storing his corn in small granaries raised upon stone 'mushrooms' (called saddle, staddle, straddle, steddle stones etc). It was the most successful way of keeping rat and corn separated because the capping stone oversailing the base prevented rodents climbing past.

Such farming practices are now largely a thing of the past and many people probably think such granaries are too, but there is a goodly scattering still surviving through the farming districts of Surrey. One came to light behind the main street of Farnham, which sounds a bit unexpected but wherever there were horses then there had to be storage facilities for their food.

This one dated from the 18th Century and was able to be saved. All the components were numbered and then transported by the Manpower Services to the Old Kiln Museum of past village life in Reeds Road, Tilford. There Mr Jackson and a builder friend used the numbers to rebuild it precisely as it was before.

It wasn't the first time it had been numbered. When the original carpenter made up the framing sections flat on the ground he numbered all the joints so that when the members were erected on their new site all the joints would match as designed. His Roman numerals can still be seen cut into the woodwork, plus the foreman's personal mark of approval.

It's a half timbered building with the panels infilled with brick. That's what it looks like anyway, but as you approach the door notice the narrow motor gap. It's not brickwork at all, but a type of tile-hanging using mathematical tiles. These were carefully designed to imitate courses of brick. They could then be used to give a fashionable new 'brick' frontage to an old house at a fraction of the cost that would otherwise be incurred.

When the joints have been grouted with mortar it's often very difficult indeed to distinguish these 'mathematical tiles' from bricks. Nevertheless, they have been identified on several Surrey houses, including one in Middle Church Lane, Farnham. It is often said that they were invented to evade the brick tax introduced in 1784 but many examples are earlier than this.

Now, on the granary at the Old Kiln Museum we have the rare chance to study this method of cladding at close quarters. Even better, you will find some loose tiles displayed inside so you can see exactly how they were designed and how they fitted together so effectively.

(17.7.87)

TITHE BARNS

"Oh yes, I'll go and draw the tithe barn," I agreed cheerily over the telephone. I wasn't so cheerful when I walked into it, at Burford Bridge Hotel, near Dorking. I knew it would be big, but I didn't think it would be THAT big!

Originally built about 1600, it was moved to Burford Bridge Hotel from Dorking in 1934. Thus it celebrates its 50th anniversary this month. Dismantling the great beams and transporting thousands of roof tiles must have been quite an undertaking.

Now it has a new lease of life. The leaded windows are sparkling free of cobwebs, the roof timbers glow and reflect in the polished surface of the dance floor, but it's all there. The double doors from the garden once let in the great wagons. The dance floor just inside was once the threshing floor. Where this extends towards the far ends was the great central aisle. This could take mountains of stooks or great ricks of hay or straw, or garage the wagons or protect the stock being overwintered. Between the aisle posts and the walls are the bays used formerly as store areas, perhaps divided off by partitions.

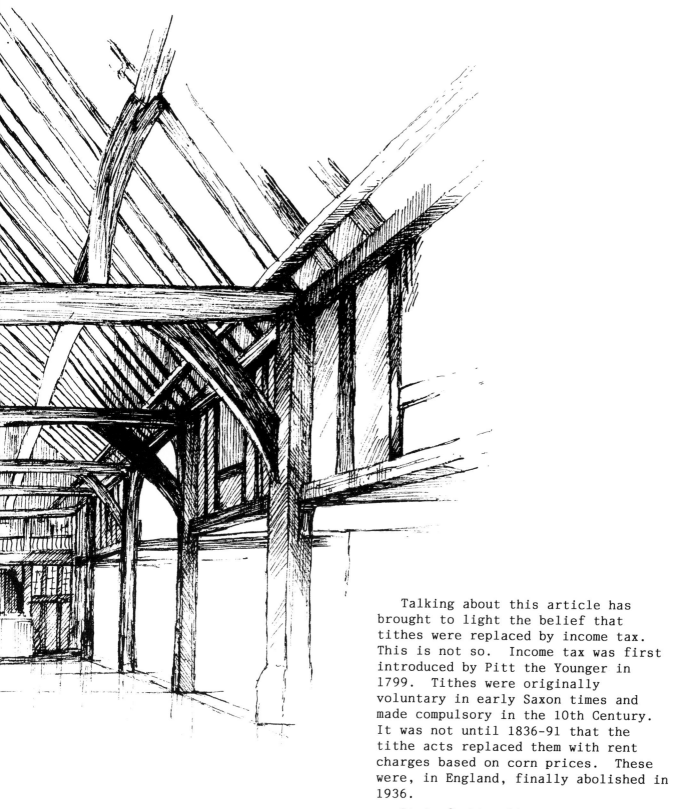

The timbering is very impressive. It's basically a series of squared up frames: vertical posts support a cross or 'tie beam'. This is further supported by angle braces. From the top of the tie beam two 'queen posts' support horizontal beams called 'purlins' which run the length of the barn halfway up the pitch of the roof. Down from the apex, over the purlins to the bottom beams run dozens of 'common rafters' which prevent the roof from sagging.

Talking about this article has brought to light the belief that tithes were replaced by income tax. This is not so. Income tax was first introduced by Pitt the Younger in 1799. Tithes were originally voluntary in early Saxon times and made compulsory in the 10th Century. It was not until 1836-91 that the tithe acts replaced them with rent charges based on corn prices. These were, in England, finally abolished in 1936.

It is fashionable to call all large barns 'tithe barns' when this might not have been so. The produce from the manorial lands had to be stored somewhere. Others were needed for the community use of the village. There was little space in the tiny squalid hovels of the workers and there were no village halls so barns served the village needs. Thus at the Burford Bridge barn there is a ministrels' gallery at one end and beneath it a fireplace, presumably for village revels.   (20.7.84)

ITALY AND ISTANBUL IN SURREY

A mile out of Wonersh and we could be in Italy, while another short distance off the M25 brings us to Istanbul. These unexpected transportations are courtesy of some of the very individual craftsmen who worked in Surrey last century.

In 1895 the squatters' hamlet of Blackheath was some 50 years old and ready for a better church. The architect brought in to do the job was C. Harrison Townsend, who isn't the best known Victorian architect. Nevertheless, he'd just attracted attention with his Bishopsgate Institute in London. Blackheath church was to be singular, too, not for being imposing and certainly not for being as modern as his institute. Instead it's a copy of the sort of roadside church found in Italy or Spain; lowly and simple.

Inside, you get a surprise because the idea is taken even as far as providing frescoes on the wall. They have a pleasant soft colouring in keeping with the general idea of the building.

To reach Istanbul turn up the London Road from its link with the M25 on top of Reigate Hill. Almost immediately you're in Lower Kingswood, but you'll hardly notice because the road is so dominant. Beside it, on the left, can be spotted the warm brick colouring of Lower Kingswood church. It's built in a Byzantine manner which is clearly hinted by the treatment of the west end.

To the north is a detached bell tower standing almost in the trees and balanced by such a large solid base that it's been shaped into steps. The little lead roof above the bell is in the Byzantine style too.

By the south wall is a very large and weathered stone capital, but none of this prepares you for the interior. The arches of the arcades spring from an amazing collection of ancient capitals brought back from Constantinople by a Dr Freshfield. There's quite a variety, from several sites, mostly dating from the 4th Century, but there's also work from the 6th and 11th Centuries too.

Apart from the interest of the stonework there's some good woodwork, evidently by the architect, Sidney Barnsley. He's continued the traditions of using the natural qualities of the timber in their own right. Thus the paleness of holly against the darkness of ebony brings a rich Eastern effect to the inlay work, and where mother-of-pearl has been used an even finer sense of the East has been achieved. It must have delighted Dr Freshfield.

It would be good to compare these with a very English example, but I cannot think of a Surrey one which is of the 1890's and has individual quality. Most of our good Victorian churches had been built by then. Of these, perhaps Holmbury St Mary is a fair choice as it was built by G E Street in 1879 at his own expense and therefore has the personal commitment so often needed for individualism.

It is certainly very English and a fine building. As with Blackheath the exterior is fairly plain and just like Kingswood the interior is rich. As you'll have gathered, I like them all, in their own particular ways.

(31.7.87)

C. Hawkins 1987
Lower Kingswood

LOOKING FOR STONE HOUSES

Early stone-built houses are a great rarity in Surrey as there's no good natural building stone. Nevertheless it was to Surrey that the medieval builders turned when working on London Bridge, Old St Paul's, Westminster Palace and Windsor Castle.

What they quarried was Reigate Firestone from under the North Downs at Merstham. Of course, the aforementioned works were all of high status and there's the clue. Surrey's quarries were worked largely in the royal service and Surrey's commoners had to do without.

The best alternative was the bargate stone of the Godalming district. Although used since Romano-British times it was never exploited fully during the medieval and Tudor periods. Timber was the accepted material and thousands of timber-framed houses still survive in Surrey to prove how good it was and how high the level of craftsmanship.

There is very little to show our craftsmanship with stone. The Cistercian monks gathered enough for their abbey at Waverley but at the Dissolution most of it was dismantled and transported to Guildford to build Loseley - our finest stone Tudor house.

Henry VIII did the same. He had Chertsey Abbey dismantled to have the material re-used for building Oatlands Palace at Weybridge and that was subsequently used again for building the locks on the Wey Navigation. The royal palace at Woking was quarried similarly, to build Hoe Place.

Looking for work of lesser status is largely to search in vain. There's the Royal Grammar School in Guildford, of course, but in the terms of houses there's one splendid example. It's the one illustrated, to be found on the roadside through those unattractive approaches to Haslemere station.

I've drawn it devoid of adjoining buildings and the commercial signs so that its smartness can be seen more clearly, as can its distinctiveness.

In a county still thick with "open hall" housing it's a valuable example of the next stage. Its compactness, central chimney and window arrangement all alert us to the new development. It has been named variously but "lobby-entry house" seems popular at the moment..

No longer does the doorway lead to a passage that divides the house in two, but into a lobby backed by the stairs and a chimney; a procedure that varied in design from house to house. Here the chimney rises from the back, so presumably the window over the door lit the stairs.

To the left of the door the single window lit the parlour. To the right the first and largest window lit the hall, which is now a much smaller room than previously. No longer is this a large communal space for numerous labourers employed on the land. Times had changed. The Tudor enclosures had created smaller holdings needing fewer workers, often little more than the family itself.

The end of the hall was partitioned off and divided into two smaller service rooms, hence the small window on the right. These again go under various names, such as milkhouse and buttery. To modern thinking they are closer to the more familiar kitchen and scullery.

Such designs originated in the early 16th Century in South East England. They spread and became almost universal in the 17th Century.

(2.8.85)

68

NEWARK PRIORY RUINS
(detail from a larger study)
which is now largely a heap
of flints and mortar since
the valuable building stone
which once encased it has
been robbed for new buildings.

HIDDEN PLACES

Driving into Godalming from Guildford takes you along Meadrow where the Wyatt Almshouses catch the eye on the left. Then past some trees and on to the road junction ... missed it!

Those trees conceal another of Surrey's remarkable but little known places of great interest. Leave the pavement and walk through the shade and up the gravelled drive to the mown grass at the end. An old flagged path leads between headstones and footstones to a long, low building and chapel stretched across the scene. To the left is a domestic cottage adjoining rooms for community use then, to the right, the range extends as a chapel.

This is the "home" of the local Unitarians. They're the second oldest non-conformist community in the area, after the Quakers. They are the first mentioned in Godalming in 1699 while their foundation on this Meadrow site dates from 1783 and the chapel from 1789. [This feature was used for the bi-centennial.]

Whether the cottage accommodation for the minister was built at the same time as the chapel or added later is a matter of some debate. Visually it prompts a later date, but the roof timbers are continuous throughout the range and when some of the cladding was removed for repair work the brick courses beneath were found to be continuous too. It's referred to in 1821, but there are earlier repair bills for such a home.

The inside of the chapel is light and airy and friendly; one big room with an added gallery for when the chapel was filled to hear the Word of God. For those who then wished to demonstrate their faith, a baptistery was provided. The floorboards can still be lifted to reveal the steps down which the faithful trod to dedicate their lives to God through a baptismal service of total immersion.

The Unitarians have no belief in Original Sin, nor the Trinity, nor that Jesus was the one and only son of God. They have no creed to fix their beliefs immovably. Thus they're a tolerant group; some take oaths while others will not. They take the Scriptures as a guide to life, enabling them to develop as individuals and be progressive as a group. They accept women as ministers and have had two at Meadrow. One, the Rev'd Mabel Beames, worked with this community for over 30 years.

As early as 1834 the Sunday school regulations forbade flogging which was very progressive in those days. If the children got bored with the service they could read the books in the church library. Going to church was not a punishing experience.

"It's all so peaceful," observed the trustees' secretary Mrs Slade, "because nobody had ever been afraid here." (11.8.89)

TRIUMPHS OF DESIGN

A recent present of a book on Britain's medieval stained glass has sent me off to look again at what we have in Surrey. Although some three dozen churches have at least some fragments remaining there is surprisingly little worth going to see. This is rather surprising as one of the chief centres of manufacture was at Chiddingfold. There they made greenish white glass which can be seen at Shere and Ockham.

It isn't known when or where coloured glass was first made in England, before the 16th Century. The earlier glass we see today would have been made in France, in Normandy. A clearer glass was made in Germany and shipped across for use in the more northern parts of the country. Wherever it came from, we have been converting it into windows since Saxon times.

The oldest in Surrey is probably at Compton although that is arguable. It is the small study of the Virgin and Child in the lower east window, thought by a few to be Norman like the setting while other experts give it a thirteenth century date. It is not easy to see it very closely so take binoculars. Nearly as old are two roundels in the east window of West Horsley church. One shows the martyrdom of St Catherine and the other shows Mary Magdalen washing Christ's feet. The third roundel, far right, is Victorian.

These are triumphs of design, especially St Catherine's roundel with its wheels within the circle: one wheel complete and isolated to remind people so clearly that by this torture she was put to death. Despite centuries of weathering the reds, blues and whites still twinkle and glow. Evidently there are 109 pieces of glass in this 12in. circle. I lost count.

Good places for beginners to start are Buckland and Worplesdon where whole panels have survived. At Byfleet some pieces have been placed in the north chancel windows where the sun cannot dazzle you. They are also fairly low and easy to see. The church is usually locked but the rectory is on the distant corner to the west.

The Byfleet panel, illustrated, shows well the glazier's art of story telling; a simple scene with the meaning emphasised by exaggeration of detail or gesture. The suppliant is obviously successful as the saint is raising his hand in blessing. A very striking face of a saint looks down from another panel, the blue Madonna with them is not medieval.

How nerve-racking it must have been for the 'glass wryghte' when his window was finally fixed into place and for the first time he could see whether he had achieved what he had imagined through all the stages of creation. No other art form is actually created by light in the way of these windows. Long may we preserve them. On that note, don't miss the message scratched into the glass at Ockham: "W. Peters new leaded this in 1775 and never was paid for the same."   (12.8.83)

STRANGERS TALKING

Many of you will recognise this week's illustration as Shalford Mill. It is so very popular with artists, but I'm not sure why. It's difficult to get a variety of viewpoint to choose from.

Standing was enforced by the fence and made it a tiring exercise. I stood in the footpath and had to move several times. Then the proportions were a curse. They're broader than in most Surrey vernacular buildings so old clever-sticks got the angel of the gable wrong and had to start again.

I moved again for an elderly man who decided he would stand behind me and wheeze. "Do you know what you're drawing?" he asked. I wasn't sure what he was getting at. I thought he was going to say he lived there and was sick to death with artists peering into his privacy.

"It's a masterpiece," he said, "a masterpiece of technology. You youngsters think you know all about technology but you don't know a thing about waterwheels. What wood do they use?" he demanded.

"Oak," I said.

"Ah, only for wet wheels," he retorted rather sharply. "Oak in the wet, 'cause it don't rot. What about the dry wheels up above?"

"Ash?" I suggested.

"No! Besh! (beech). They use besh 'cause it's got spring in it. Don't want them cogs sheering off do you? One snaps and you lose dozens."

"What happens then?" I queried as I lost count of the courses of tiles I was drawing.

"You has to fit new ones and quick - if mill don't work it don't earn you any money. No fixed wages in my youth, you know."

You drive the old tenon out and drive a new one in, with a sledge hammer. We made our own. Tricky business - got to be shaped perfect to fit the mortice, must line up with centre of wheel."

"Can't you cut them from a pattern?" I asked.

"No lad, they've got to match up with those on t'other wheel and if them's worn out you've got to compensate. You make 'em too big. Then you pares off where the sledge has burred the top. Then you work on back and front 'cause they're different. Then you measure 'em for length."

He was now sounding well satisfied as though he'd just finished a perfect job on a challenging wheel. I'd given up drawing by this time. He went on about measuring length which I didn't quite understand. The basic idea was that they are not measured from the rim of the wheel, nor from the centre but from the wheel above by turning one wheel into the other. The successful marriage of the two was the crucial point and therefore they were measured against each other. The bit I didn't understand involved measuring from a fixed point above in order to reduce the cog to a size that would fit. As the fit had to be exact this was crucial but he wasn't keen to repeat himself. I was accused of not listening!

Listening, he asserted, was vital. "If you don't listen you don't knows you got it right. If they don't fit proper they shout at you. Now, you do your picture."

(30.8.85)

73

ADDED ATTRACTIONS AT HATCHLANDS

Outside, the heat reflected up from the paved terrace with a rich scent of lavender. Inside, all was cool and free from sharp light and bright colours. No doubt the contrast was just as much appreciated by Admiral Boscowan after a hard ride over the park to this, his home, at Hatchlands.

It has been in the care of the National Trust for some time but only recently has it been possible to open it fully to the public. Much work has been undertaken to ensure a visit is worthwhile. Thus all through last winter [1987-88] a further extensive programme of repair, refurbishment and redecoration was undertaken in readiness for receiving furniture and paintings from the collection of Mr Alec Cobbe.

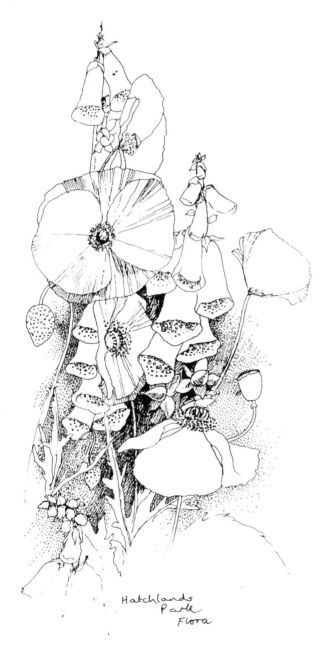

Hatchlands
Park
Flora

He also collected something else - keyboard instruments - and it's these which add so much to the new distinction of Hatchlands, especially as some are not to be seen elsewhere in Britain. Don't imagine boring ranks drawn up like expectant taxis; they're dotted through the rooms among the furnishings just as they were originally.

I'm no musician, but the temptation did cross my mind to lift a lid and have a quick "tinkle." Fear not, I restrained myself! If, however, you are a serious musician you can enjoy the privilege of playing on two of the instruments, by simply making an appointment. Alternatively, you may be lucky enough to visit on a day when professional players are giving demonstration performances but you'll have to take pot-luck for that. Nevertheless, developing the potential of Hatchlands for pleasing music-lovers is now one of the aims of the National Trust.

Picture-lovers are well catered for too, as Mr Cobbe is a restorer by profession. Over 80 paintings furnish the walls at present including such masters as Rubens and Gainsborough. Over and around them remains the treasure for which Hatchlands has always been noted: the earliest decorative scheme of Robert Adam.

The house certainly has much to offer, but the gardens have been neglected. Not for long; restoration work is due to begin soon. Of particular interest to Surrey people is the parterre, designed by Surrey's most noted gardener, Gertrude Jekyll. It's the only example of her work in the county regularly open to the public.

There's also the 18th century garden temple rescued from Busbridge Hall nestling against the trees. What trees they are too, whether it's the spreading oaks in the surrounding pastures completing the image of an English country park or the enormous plane tree on the lawn or the young tulip trees etc. planted to enhance the grounds further, for future generations.   (9.9.88)

[Since then, work has progressed apace, both in the house and in restoring the Jekyll garden and the park.]

18thC. Temple
Clandon ~ Hatchlands
C. Hawkins 1988.

WALTER OF OCKHAM

This week's face is that of Walter Frilende. I haven't been cruel with my pen - it's just that he's been dead since 1354. I copied the face from his memorial brass in Ockham Church but even that is not a portrait. True portraits on brasses are exceptionally rare. It would have been the case that somewhere, possibly in London, the next item on the craftsman's job list was to make a demi-figure of a priest. Thus, with his burin he gouged out of the latten plate a face - any old face.

It's also rare in Surrey for us to know who built our medieval churches and who paid for them. We do know, however, that this Walter was one. He paid for the north aisle of Ockham Church to be rebuilt as the chapel of St Margaret.

The arcade (illustrated) or arches and pillar that separates the nave from the north aisle is as Walter knew it, but minus its paint. It is standard 13th century work which led to an earlier aisle. Walter demolished that and built the one in use today. Even if this face isn't a portrait it does remind us that we are not just looking at architecture, but at the ideas and skills of real people who really lived. Quite probably Walter's face really was a bit haggard. He was known to King Edward III and worked for the Court - always a dangerous juggling ground of one power against another. He is described as the "King's Clerk," which has been interpreted as being a civil servant for the exchequer. It is also thought that he may have been a local. I wonder how a country lad became so successful.

The clue comes from his local patron, the Earl of Stafford. There's a reminder of him too, in the church. In the south-west window of the chancel, around the edge, the Stafford Knot is worked in stained glass. It has a beautiful greenish hue that indicates that the glass was almost certainly made at the famous glass centre of Chiddingfold in the south of the county.

Walter became rector in 1349. It was just two years before that the Staffords came into the story when Ralph married a local lady and paid relief for her lands. The Staffords' stories take us to battles at Shrewsbury and Northampton and also to the scaffold.

In 1528 Henry VIII ended the connection by giving the Manor to John Bourchier, Lord Berners. To follow that up we need to go to West Horsley.

(14.9.84)

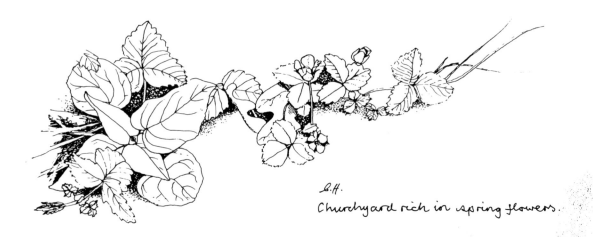

G.H.
Churchyard rich in spring flowers.

COTTAGE LIFE - OAKHURST

After the grandeur of Hatchlands last time to the smallest of the National Trust houses this time but it's still absolutely grand.

Oakhurst Cottage, at Hambledon, is so tiny that viewing is by appointment only, but it's well worth that moment of forward planning. Here you can click a garden gate and walk up the path between "old-fashioned" garden flowers to see inside one of those half-timbered Tudor cottages that are so much part of the Surrey countryside; so much part of the foreigners' view of England.

Inside there's just a main living-room and two tiny rooms leading off, all squeezed into a small building which is thought to have started life as a barn because it was designed without an upper floor. That's proven by the cutaway beams in the bedrooms and up the stairs, all added back in Jacobean times. Since then it's only had very minor alterations, like moving the bread oven.

In true National Trust style it is maintained and presented not as a museum but as a home. Some half-finished knitting lies on the fireside chair, as though left by the lady to open the door. Nearby stands her besom broom of heather after the round of daily chores and all the while the herbs continue drying in their suspended bunches ready for the next meal.

It'll be a cold meal today; the fire in its wide open hearth isn't lit, so there's the tingling smell of soot - a nostalgic smell for those too long cocooned in central heating.

There are no modern conveniences here. Everything is furnished as it would have been in the last century. You'll be shown round the "conveniences", the tinder-box for striking a light, the handmade candles (genuine, from the Ironbridge Museum complex) and the bedwarmer. Then there's the curious wooden tub with an even odder implement which is the "washing machine"! The water, of course, comes from the well in the garden, round the other side from the bee skeps. Even further off are the toilet facilities!

It's full of the curious. At least they are the genuine West Surrey household items. They come from the collection made by Gertrude Jekyll. Some, like the mouse-trap, you may already have seen photographed in her "Old West Surrey".

Best of all is the way the National Trust has cleverly underplayed the whole idea. It doesn't give the impression of being preserved, but leaves you with the feeling that the family are simply out, due to return later, that the knitting will be finished when the children are all piled into the bed upstairs and, come another day, the besom will flick away the autumn leaves from the threshold.

(23.9.88)

ARTIST AMONG

THE FILM-MAKERS

A chance sighting of a drawing poking out of a mass of material being prepared for public display in Chertsey Museum led Seen in Surrey into fresh pastures.

Seeing my interest, the curator pulled out photographs of lovely old timber buildings; just the sort I love to draw. They looked like my idea of the Australian outback, but evidently came from America's cowboy country. Then there was a set of drawings of them; drawings beautifully accurate yet not fussy, vigorous but not casual. Soon I was being shown how these were being built up to create a street scene followed by a photograph of a model. That gave the game away; no backs - it was for a film set. More photographs showed the "real" street populated with familiar figures from the silver screen acting out The Sheriff of Fractured Jaw(1957). It was the work of Bernard Robinson, who came to live in Chertsey in 1958 until his death in 1970.

"He wanted everything to be absolutely authentic, not the usual Hollywood sham," Mrs Robinson explained to me, as she went on to recall the experiences of making the film. That was in Spain. He'd insisted the road be built properly and it was. The Spanish were so pleased with it they kept it. He'd a way with Spanish workmen, too, which got the work done. There were memories of the film stars, of course, and of the Indians - real American Indians were brought over especially. Everything had to be authentic.

Tales and memories and comments slipped gently into the quiet of the exhibition room and gradually reassembled into Bernard Robinson. Around us, the walls were lined with his oil paintings, looking as fresh as when he'd just finished them. Through the door, the stairway was lined with a very different set of paintings. These were of local scenes.

"He loved to get out into the Surrey lanes and enjoy painting," Mrs Robinson was saying, and it showed. They were all very different in style from the work for the film studios. He worked on no fewer than 76 films, among them such classics as Carve Her Name with Pride and Reach for the Sky, the story of Douglas Bader which gained him an Oscar nomination. Chiefly, though, he created the Hammer Horrors, with Dracula, Frankenstein, Quatermass, Vampires and Zombies.

It was certainly going to make a very interesting exhibition and at the same time will be shown the paintings and intriguing puppets created by another artist, the lady he married. As she reminisced over tea in the exhibition room the gap in the curtains let sunlight catch her white hair and light her rounded smiling features and the smile in her eyes. She was calm and gentle but as an artist she's still experimenting with new ideas and new materials urging and persuading them to create the effect that she wants.   (25.9.87)

VILLAGE COTTAGES

Looking around Seale and finding buildings of chalk reminded me of making this illustration a couple of years ago, where the main cottage was also built from blocks of chalk.

There are few such buildings in the county despite the North Downs stretching right across Surrey. This is due to the softness of the material which, although ideal for cutting into building blocks, has a low resistance to weathering. Indeed, the chalk beds of Surrey are particularly soft. Neighbouring counties have been more fortunate.

The low quality restricted its use largely to humbler cottages and farm buildings and these have since perished. Survivors do not usually pre-date the 17th Century, although chalk walls were in use in medieval times and indeed go right back to prehistoric times. The real problems arose not so much from the faces of the walls but from any corners left exposed to the weather. These had to be protected and reinforced by the use of a tougher material. Stone was ideal but was so scarce in Surrey as to add considerably to the cost. These were, after all, envisaged as cheaper grade buildings. In these cases our great standby was brick; quoins, jambs and lintels in the illustrated cottage are all in cherry red brick. It contrasts smartly with pale walls. Of course there was another way of shielding the softness from the weather and that was to clad all exterior surfaces.

Not surprisingly, the examples illustrated are by the canal. Water transport was ideal for shifting heavy materials. The Wey Navigation transported much chalk, not just as a building material but also as agricultural fertiliser. Nationally, the canals promoted the use of Welsh slate as a roofing material from the late 18th Century. These cottages at Broadford have slate and so do some of the Seale examples but these are thanks to the railways rather than a canal.

It is no surprise to find chalk used at Seale as it had its own great chalkpit. A wide range of other materials were also used to create the village, in a typical Surrey way. The eye catches Manor House Farm, thrusting a great chalk building towards the approach from Farnham while the next building is a nice contrast with its typical Surrey weather-boarding. Then comes a surprise, just round the corner, Stable Cottage built of chalk but on a very ambitious scale compared with usual. The adjoining terrace sticks to the well-tried Surrey brick and very attractive it is, too. Already the colour shows that Farnham is being left behind, for the clays from that direction fired to a more orange colour.

Still moving along towards the church, the next building of note is a farmhouse set back in isolation. It's left hand end wall is built of local ironstone, culled from the outcrops of sandstone to the south, away from the Downs. It's the sort of wall seen more often in East Surrey, in the Limpsfield area, while the local sandstone is a darker, richer brown than that from Godalming quarries. It's more like the Wealden sandstones used south of Dorking, in places like the church tower at Capel. It looks good here in Seale church.

Broadford
Waterside.

Wotton, Surrey
August 1986

Skenfrith, Gwent
August 86

WOTTON'S WELSH CONNECTION

"Welcome to Wales" says a little church tower over Dorking way. It's Wotton's. The Welsh connection is in its design, for the tower rises in two stages, the upper being of a smaller plan than the tower base. The discrepancy is bridged by roofing all around. Hopefully you can see better what I mean from the sketch.

As many books point out, this is a design usually found in Gwent of which Skenfrith is the most notable. As I drive through there quite often, I stopped and sketched it for comparison. Although the proportions are different the basic design is the same. The church at Clun, in Shropshire has such a tower too. It's better to think of it as a Welsh borderlands design than truly Welsh.

The occurrence of the design at Wotton is often remarked upon as odd. Is it really so? Look at the history of the manor and who do you find taking over from one Oswold, a saxon, but Richard de Tonbridge? That great Surrey landowner from the reign of William the Conqueror was the founder of the House of de Clare and the de Clares were Lords of the March between Wales and England. Surely, it is through them that the design came to Surrey.

The lower parts of the tower at Wotton may be Saxon. The Victoria County History suggests c.1050 and gives reasons, all of which are in keeping with less dubious Saxon claims from other churches. The Buildings of England prefers an early Norman date, as that series tends to do. Whatever the exact date, the important point seems to be that the top is later and that the "foreign" design was adapted to fit an existing tower. Hence the taller, narrower proportions than those at Clun and Skenfrith.

The latter is a delightful village if you are Gwent way. The street faces the castle, with river cum moat cum millpool behind and the church at the end with lots of grassy spaces all about. Very different is Wotton with no village street at all. A little lane off the main road runs down on to a spur over a deep coombe. Down there it's really countryside: hills and deep valleys, woods and fields. Of course, it's especially fine now in October when the leaves on the hanger are changing colour.

Among the rough grass of the churchyard you'll find the headstones of the Vaughan-Williams family (of composer fame but related to Charles Darwin and Josiah Wedgwood for good measure). Their association comes from Leith Hill Place which came into their ownership in 1847. Other people will associate Wotton with John Evelyn, the diarist, whose family home was here. John himself requested not to be buried in the family mausoleum attached to the church, but that is exactly where he is. (10.10.86)

CHILWORTH FOR GUNPOWDER AND PAPER

Take the lane that links Chilworth to Merrow via St Martha's and where you cross the Tillingbourne you'll find the scene illustrated. The drawing was made as the new growth spurted up and the woods were rich with bluebell scent. It's a rewarding area to explore at any time, though.

This lovely old Surrey building, for instance, used to be rag-house for the paper mill. All around are other buildings with an industrial history, mostly concerning the manufacture of gunpowder. What all seems so peaceful today was bustling with an estimated 600 workers, employed here during the First World War. Many of the workforce were not employed directly at gunpowder manufacturing, but at support jobs such as coopering all the barrels needed for transporting the powder. Only a few men would go near the production areas when they were functioning because of the danger from explosion. Thus the safety record is surprisingly good.

Bad days are still marked by craters in the woods. The explosions could be heard in Guildford and an observer away on Hindhead happened to witness one, judging from his description, which makes it like an H-bomb cloud.

Storage magazines were tucked inside great U-shaped mounds which can still be spotted, as can other banks for blast protection. Then there are the "Chilworth Mounds," which are rolls of corrugated iron filled with earth, and so effective as to have been adopted all round the world.

Alas, one day, this simple but valuable invention will rust away in the woods that have since grown up here. Most of the main buildings have gone or are in ruins. In fact, many walkers must think them an "eyesore" unless they understand their importance. There are old waterways, half-buried railway tracks and millstones to look out for too. Even if the industrial archaeology of paper and gunpowder doesn't excite you, the walk in the trees here is very attractive. Enter from Blacksmith Lane beside a cottage (which used to be the West Lodge of the site). On your left you'll find my sketching spot.

The scene has more interest than appears at first. The mill pond shown has another to the right, upstream. Here was once a hopfield to satisfy the workers' thirst! Water from this pond has to escape down a culvert that goes right underneath the lower pond. The paper and gunpowder manufacturers using this site were not ideal neighbours. The former were anxious lest the latter should fill the air with burning debris!

The paperworkers moved out; the Unwin family business moved to Old Woking where their Gresham Press still flourishes. The gunpowder workers moved out, too, when demand fell after the First World War. So the site went into another cycle of change that continues today. It is well documented and explained in A Guide to the Chilworth Gunpowder Mills, by Glenys Crocker.   (11.10.85)

Town House

C. Harkins.
Town House
Haslemere

ROBBING CURATE

Guiding people around Haslemere as a place of interest is no easy matter. There's plenty to generalise over and the townscape design of the High Street is attractive with its backing of hills. The buildings, however, tend to stare back blankly. Surprisingly few help to bring the past to life. One where several notable people lived is Town House, in the High Street, opposite the Museum.

It recalls local traditions, attributed to a number of parishes, concerning a certain cleric whose cassock sometimes bulged over what looked suspiciously like pistol butts; a cleric who always ended services on those occasions with long hymns - long enough for him to defrock in the vestry and ride off on his horse kept tethered outside. Parishioners got no farewell from their curate at the church door on those occasions.

People began to think he might be their local highwayman; after all, his standard of living was high for a cleric, but then again he was also the local magistrate and just as vexed by the highway robberies as anyone else.

The Haslemere version of this story links the Gentleman with Town House where The Rev'd James Fielding lived between 1772 and 1784. He died in 1817 and soon slipped from people's thoughts, until that is, later renovations to Town House involved lifting the floorboards. There they discovered a stash of 18th century mail bags complete with brass identity tags. These connected the bags with the robberies and revived memories of The Rev'd James Fielding. He had been buried at Haslemere's parish church of St Bartholomew in an unmarked vault, probably under what is now the main path.

The church stands well away from the town centre and to reach it the cleric would have needed to cross a valley with pools and marshes and mill ponds. These were all drained away when it was decided to drive the railway through this natural cutting (Haslemere is the highest point on the line). The name of Tanners Lane reminds us of those earlier industrial days.

The church area is not unattractive with its sloping green, planted long ago with horse chestnut trees, backed by the large early 18th century Church Hill House. To the north, the church rooms are housed in the former church school: a little gothic building that would complement the scene so much more if its old play areas were enhanced.

Between them stands the church, rebuilt in 1871. Ignore its description as 'hopeless' until you've seen it for yourself. The long chancel with tall narrow lancet windows demonstrates more clearly the 13th century stereotype than any of the originals surviving in Surrey. At the west end the original tower was retained. It is so devoid of detail that it is difficult to date but is probably 13th century. It's more like a defensive refuge tower and indeed that may well have been in its builders' minds for in those days it was a chapel of Chiddingfold, lost out in the remote forested hills; not the securest place to live.

The interior is not a Victorian glory except perhaps in its hopelessness. The font in gaudy coloured marble says it all as soon as you enter but says it more brazenly than any other in the country. The stained glass doesn't merit comment either, although one window in the north aisle, designed but Burne-Jones, attracts visitors because it is a memorial to the local Poet Laureate, Alfred, Lord Tennyson.   (20.10.89)

Green Place
Wonersh
1986-7

A family of 25 children isn't bad going and so we can be certain that infant mortality reduced that number before they were recorded as part of their parents' memorial brass.

Dad died on June 2, 1503. He was Henry Elyot, of Wonersh, and there in the parish church the brass survives showing Henry, his wife Joan, 12 sons and 11 daughters. No attempt at portraiture was attempted; the figures are symbolic. Accurate detailing was, however, often commissioned for detailing of costume or heraldry that would signify status.

Thus this memorial brass was provided with two shields of arms at the top, possibly duplicated at the bottom until the matrix was reduced in size. Henry's family arms would have been on his side and Joan's on hers, but they no longer survive. That's a pity because they would have settled whether Joan was of the Wintershull family, as tradition says.

Even without these and without taking the cost of such a memorial into account, it is clear that the Elyots were of note. The engraver was instructed to edge Henry's gown with fur and to line the hood with more while the front lappet of Joan's head-dress is richly patterned. No wonder Henry has to carry a dagger concealed behind the purse on his belt. They had muggers in those days, too!

They were one of the two great families of Wonersh and had been so since the 14th Century. From their times other links have survived.

Their home, for example, was the half-timbered portion of Green Place which still stands, nearly opposite the church. Henry had been given it by his father, Thomas, whose memorial brass is also in the church. This one gives us a clearer indication of the source of the family's wealth for the inscription records (in Latin) that he was filacer for Surrey and Sussex in the court of King's bench and Clerk of the peace for Surrey. As filacer his responsibility was to file the writs in the courts. These were the last Elyots to live at Green Place, for Henry sold it and moved out to Busbridge Hall nearer Godalming.

How Henry maintained the family doesn't seem to be known but it is thought he was involved in the local wool trade. Certainly he is shown in civilian dress like other wool merchants, but that's no proof. Even his father is shown thus without any badge of office or livery.

Other houses he would have known are still standing along the village street, even if a little disguised by 19th century usage. Out in Lord's Hill Road is Yieldhurst where, it's suggested, one of the guilds associated with the woollen trade was based and it was the local guild which probably had the north chapel added to the parish church for its specific use. The villagers who prompted this feature also related that woad, grown for its blue dye, persists as a weed in their Wonersh gardens. (23.10.87)

THE RIVER WEY

A recent book on Surrey says: "The River Wey rises in Hampshire." That's only half the truth. There are two main sources, only one of which is in Hampshire (near Selbourne). It is an important one because it springs from the water table of the chalk downs and that immense reservoir is usually able to maintain a constant flow.

The other source is in West Sussex, on the south flank of Blackdown, behind Haslemere. Find Cotchet Farm (Map ref 914296) and behind the farm lane there's a cattle trough, overflowing into a ditch. Follow the water upstream a few yards and you'll find it splashing down through the roots under the bole of a great tree on the hillside. It sounds romantic, but that's the way it is.

Instead of flowing south into the Weald and becoming one of the tributaries of the River Arun, it flows westwards into Hampshire as far as Bordon and then north to Surrey at Frensham and so to Tilford. There it joins the other branch from Selbourne. Tilford is one of those places where one is very conscious of the river because access to the village green has to be negotiated over two very narrow medieval bridges.

Then there's one at Elstead - not the bridge by the village centre which is later, (probably 16th century) but another by Somerset Farm, and thus often referred to as Somerset Bridge.

Their age is unknown as they lack architectural detail. They do, however, have semi-circular arches which have led some books to state they were build by the Normans. When it comes to simple country bridges, the changes in fashion were less important than the cost so the lack of Gothic pointed arches is no certain indication of date. The cost and the maintenance usually fell to the landowners of each bank, their responsibilities meeting in the centre of the bridge. This was not a harmonious arrangement, as you can imagine.

With Tilford, the responsibility would have fallen upon Waverley Abbey. Its annals record great floods in 1233, damaging local bridges. Thus this series may date from repairing and rebuilding at this time, following the earlier style with semi-circular arches.

C. Hawkins
8.86

They're only 11.5 ft wide, like the similar one at Unstead. They form part of a series of six early bridges along the Wey. The others are wider at 13-14 ft and include the well-known Eashing Bridge. Over the mill-stream at Eashing there is a second one.

It's not the arches, however, that we should look at but the cut-waters. On the downstream side they are semi-circular in plan and that makes them very special because nowhere else was this design adopted. Why our bridges should have this peculiarity has not been explained. (7.11.86)

West Molesey

TRENDY NEW WINDOWS

The recent features on William
Wykeham, Bishop of Winchester,
certainly brought some responses,
especially for not mentioning
Effingham Church. It was one that had
to be repaired when the bishop
discovered that Merton Priory had not
been maintaining the churches in its
care.

That was in 1388, the year after
work had begun on his new college at
Winchester. For that important
development the master mason was
William Wynford who made his name
developing a new style of
architecture. We now call that
perpendicular; the only major
contribution that England has made to
the world history of art, according to
John Harvey, the authority on the
style.

The work of these two great men can
be seen at Effingham. The north and
south walls of the chancel contain
very distinctive windows, best seen
from the outside so it doesn't matter
if the church is locked. The chancel
is indeed where we would expect to
find them because that part of the
fabric was the responsibility of the
clergy, whereas the parishioners had
the care of the nave.

What is so special about the
windows is that they are in the new
style created at Winchester only
months before.

Although William Wykeham provides
an interesting link with all that was
going on it still doesn't explain how
the design got to Effingham. Maybe a
drawing was provided for a local
craftsman. Precious few medieval
masons' plans have survived and do not
seem to have been in regular use.
More durable on site was a board or
metal plate bearing the design, but
these weren't worth keeping either,
once fashion had changed. They may
have used full-sized ones on which to
lay the cut stones to check for
accuracy before erection. The design
marked out on cloth would have been
easiest to transport around the
country.

Alternatively, a mason may have
been sent from Winchester to do the
job or a local mason may have been
sent down there to learn the new
forms. It is even possible for the
windows to have been bought ready cut
at Winchester and transported back in
kit form. Purbeck Marble fonts of the
previous century arrived in Surrey in
kit form.

By whatever means, this new
'Perpendicular style' found favour and
spread widely. The flint and
freestone tower of the Church of St
John the Evangelist, Stoke-next-
Guildford, must be a familiar landmark
to many readers. The ragstone tower
at West Molesey less so. On the
whole, Surrey was not building new
churches at this time and so the only
large exercise in this style is right
over in Lingfield, dating from 1431.
Much nearer is the Slyfield aisle of
15th century work is integrated with
modern and 13th century architecture
and is not easy to sort out.

(8.11.85)

HYDON FOR SUCCESS

When it comes to getting new plants to offer gardeners there are the two options of either going abroad to search for something worthwhile among wild flowers, or, to stay at home and develop new ones through breeding and selection.

The second option was explained to me by Mr George of Hydon Nursery at Hascombe. He is a national authority on Rhododendrons but does not go abroad for his seed. Others do that, like Tony Schilling and Tom Spring Smythe. Some of their seed collection gets sent to Mr George, via Kew, because he has the knowledge, skill and facilities to germinate the seed and rear the new stock plants.

These are watched carefully from little seedlings up to the flowering stage with a view to selecting strong, disease-resistant strains. At flowering time Mr George's skills really come to the fore. It is then he uses his expert eye to select specimens to cross-fertilise by hand in the hope that the seed will grow into exciting hybrids, worthy of our gardens.

Public taste changes so fresh demands continually arise. Rhododendrons flourish in the acid regions of Surrey; they could well be our "county flower". Many of their admirers only have a tiny garden, though, and so currently the emphasis is upon producing Rhododendrons to suit. Small size, compact habit, attractive foliage, abundant bloom - what a challenge!

Nevertheless, Mr George has a fine record of achievement. If your little beauty at home has got 'Hydon' as a proname you will have one of these successes. If you have 'Hydon Dawn' you have the most popular of all. Only some of his hybrids carry the Hydon name. Now he is working on a good yellow for us and on new Yakushinianum hybrids.

Work it is, too, for not only is there the raising of fresh seed but also the propagation of fields of stock plants for us to buy in the autumn. Then there is all the promotion work, culminating in the Chelsea Flower Show. My visit to Mr George was immediately after Chelsea when the team were unloading their exhibition plants, but already their thoughts were turned to next year.

Rhododendron jasminiflorum 'Taylori'

The stock is watched all summer for promising exhibits budding up well. Next March these will be lifted and brought in from the fields. They have their balls of roots wrapped carefully and are kept in this way. Then comes the real skill - persuading them to burst into flower exactly on time for Chelsea.

This is achieved by temperature control. They go into greenhouses to warm them to 45 deg F, but are put out again if they are progressing too quickly. The amount of water they receive is vital, too. These variables are juggled from March till May so that the Rhododendrons will burst into bloom for judging day. Such perfection quite astonishes me; even more so when I learned this was achieved by touch. Mr George feels the buds. Their degree of stickiness is his clock. From it, he can judge their rate of progress. Now there's real craftsmanship for you!

(9.11.84)

WHERE AUTHOR WROTE HER FAMOUS NOVEL

It was not a very pleasant spot to sit and draw, beside a busy road, on a hill at a bend. It was difficult to reflect upon the cottage's younger days before bitumen when it was only the occasional cart that rattled dust out of pot-holes. There were fields all around and a stream at the bottom. Beyond stood a mill with its hammer ponds on the brink of the opposite hill, and then woods sliding down from the heights of Marley behind. It's all there still, but so is a lot more, including the railway embankment blocking all that view.

So with my back against the garden wall of Cherrimans I tried to draw the entrance to Brookbank and thought about Mr and Mrs Gilchrist who lived there in the middle of the last century. They had been captured by the fascination of William Blake and Mr Gilchrist set about writing a notable book on the man. Old Gilchrist died before he finished it, but his wife completed the task.

Meanwhile, Cherrimans was having its usual summer visitors and these included a Mr and Mrs Lewes. They weren't really married, but I don't know whether their neighbours knew that at the time. They liked the spot, especially the country walks. Thus it came about that they were able to return by renting Brookbank opposite for a summer.

Between six and eight every evening George and Mary would go walking, usually up the valleys on to the flanks of Hindhead. In the mornings it was a different matter. That was when Mary did her writing.

If we were able to slip through the gate and go round the side of the cottage we'd find her at the window on to the verandah, pad on knee, feet on a hot water bottle, all shrouded in thick clothing. Mary felt the cold. Only when everyone else was complaining about the heat would she concede to feeling a little warmth and venture to work in the garden, urged on by George.

It was he who had encouraged her to write fiction in the first place and, by praising the results, encouraged her to continue. By now they had been "connected", as he described their relationship, for fifteen years. Another secret was her identity as a writer. Some of the local people were also writers and they knew who they had in their midst.

One was Alfred, Lord Tennyson who spent the summers at the house he had built near by on Blackdown. He and his wife entertained the Leweses, and, by some accounts Mary and Alfred argued. However, there is no sign of this in Alfred's own account of the day which is very amicable. Tennyson's fear of strangers propagated many such stories.

Anyway, Mary finished writing the manuscript and upon its publication it became a great success. In order that it be taken seriously she hid behind the man's name of "George Eliot". The book was 'Middlemarch', hence the name of the right-hand part of Brookbank.

Mary Ann Evans was born today, November 22, in 1819.   (22.11.85)

FROM CART SHED TO GALLERY

It's not often that I arrange to meet someone in a cart shed, but such was the case on a recent sunny afternoon. The countryside was beautiful as I passed down through Bramley and turned left off the A281 into Whipley Manor Farm at Palmers Cross.

Beyond the farmyard was a half-timbered house with dazzling white plaster in the sunshine. Beyond that the ground fell away into the lowland before the rich textured slopes of the Leith Hill range. To the right the view was blocked by the cart shed - built in the days when care was taken over such humble buildings.

Local stone, brick, tile and weatherboarding had been brought together with pleasing proportions and a smart hipped roof. It's the sort of little building that could so easily be lost, but not here. The Whipley Manor Farm site has already won three conservation awards. Now the old cart shed has been saved.

From January to March Mr Tim Clarke worked on restoration and converting the interior to give it a new lease of life, so that by March it was ready to open - as a picture framing centre and art gallery, specialising in country pictures, principally water-colours. Their freshness is matched by the clean white walls and carpeted floor.

It's a far cry from its earlier uses, yet care has been taken to preserve the original structure. Foremost is the chief roof beam stretching across the gallery. You can see it was made from a whole tree, with the sapwood left on and soft enough for wood beetles to riddle with holes. You can also see that the oak heartwood was too hard for them. To prompt your imagination further, notice the little alcoves in the side walls. These are said to have been for storing the grease pots for lubricating the cart axles.

The end walls were once open to the weather but now one has been glazed to allow light to flood the work area for picture framing while the other, away from the strongest light, is only glazed to light the picture displays. Running right across the gallery is another carefully preserved relic feature. It's the wall that was necessary for a period when the cart shed was used to house pigs, hence the change in level. When we hear so many fears expressed that we are losing too many of our traditional countryside buildings it is good to report this one being saved and given a new lease of life.

The gallery number is 0483 268310.

(30.11.90)

SAVING TREES

It's not every day a lady rescues a complete holly tree from the bulldozers but that was the content of a recent letter. For the past 40 years she's been driving the A3 from Jackson's Corner, next to the Compton bend, to Milford and enjoyed the roadside plantings, especially of Silver Birches and Lombardy Poplars. Now the A3 is being upgraded and as she watched the rows of pegs being put in to mark out future work she noticed that some of her favourite trees were between the pegs and obviously going to be destroyed. That was too much.

Off she went to the contractors to ask if they'd "get their digger machine to dig out the whole root of a whole holly tree, about 20ft high, instead of bulldozing it down and burning it." I could imagine what the contractors had to say about that, but no, on turning the page I read that they "were very helpful and courteous."

The problem was not with the contractors but "to get a big enough lorry with a crane on it, to arrive at the right moment, and again they were very co-operative and held up the digging job - so that it would come straight out of the ground, on to the lorry and into the great hole I had dug for it by our front gate."

That hole at home had been another problem, solved by a neighbour with a digger. He excavated one ten feet across and six feet deep. In due course the Holly arrived and was duly planted.

"The only sad thing, she added, "is that it is a bit disorientated, as the way the crane picked it up and put it into the hole allowed only very little manipulation and it had to go into the hole back to front, which means the north side is now facing south."

Consequently the tree lost much of its foliage as Hollies do not like their trunks exposed to the sun; the smooth thin bark is poor protection from the direct rays. Normally they grow in the shade and broken sunlight of open woodland and protect themselves with a further dense surround of their own evergreen leaves. Nevertheless, this particular one recovered from its shock and by the time I went to see it all the tips were alive and well with a new year's growth on them.

Hopefully it will berry again soon, as it was when it arrived. Even green holly is appreciated at this time of the year and was given, in the past, by country employers as part of their Christmas bonus to their workmen. Gertrude Jekyll recorded a retired worker saying of his former boss: "After I left, there was always a bit of green holly at Christmas ..."

(15.12.89)

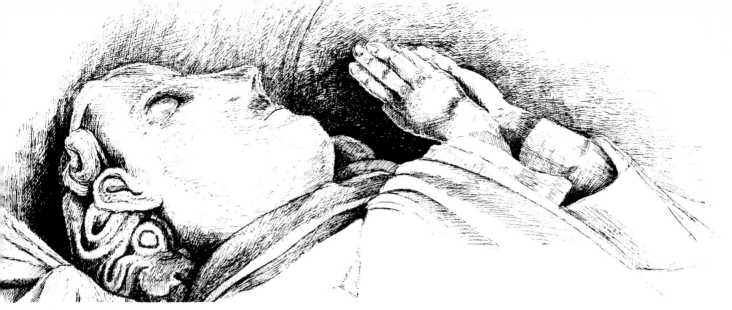

HORSLEY'S STONE MAN

Lying in the north chancel wall of the church at West Horsley is the solid stone effigy of a priest. If deductions are right this is Ralph de Berners and he's resting in a church he served.

Surrey has few tomb effigies so he's rather special, and more so for probably being the earliest. He's said to date from "about 1377," but how you can prefix such a precise date without "about" I'm not sure. It puts the work into the Decorated period of art history and there's not much of that in Surrey either, so the whole tomb recess is worth a look.

The arch is pinnacled as you would expect but look at the base of the pinnacles and you'll find little carvings of animal heads. They look like pigs to me but perhaps they're dogs. On the other hand, if this is indeed a Berners tomb, then they will be monkey heads off the family heraldry.

Such effigies regularly have sculpture to support the feet, such as lions for knights and angels for priests. Ralph is shown as a vested priest and a quick glance reveals he has an angel at his feet, but you look over its back. There's a tail! It's the sort of tail a lion might have. It's certainly not what I'd expect an angel to have. Perhaps it's a Berners monkey tail.

Most of the sculpture is well preserved. The face is big and bold; the subtleties were painted on. The hands were broken off at some date and early guides refer to them as lying loose in the back of the recess. This century they have been cemented back on.

The Berners family had a long association with West Horsley. In 1271 a Ralph de Berners was granted the manor by Hugh de Windsor. The latter was descended from the holder listed in the Doomsday Book and his daughter is thought to have been the Christina who was married to Ralph. The manor passed through the female heirs several times before it passed out of the family in 1518 on being mortgaged to Thomas Unton.

Christina nominated a certain Roger de Berners as rector, This was unfortunate as Edward III held the right of presentation. Anyway, the Bishop of Winchester was ordered by the archbishop to institute Roger. He did. Then in 1317 he had to remove him for neglecting the church and rectory. Worse still, he'd got married!

Another member of the family to err was Christina's great-grandson, James, who inherited the manor in 1361. He was still a boy then but grew up to be influential in the government of another boy - King Richard II, who was only eleven when he came to the throne. We can see an image of this James Berners, as a knight of the realm, kneeling in the stained glass window above the tomb. There too is the monkey again!

James was accused of taking advantage of the youthful king and this was his downfall. He was beheaded in 1388 and his lands were taken by the Crown. James's wife petitioned the king to get back the West Horsley estates and in this she was successful. Edward IV later confirmed the arrangement but had a good moan about Parliament not having been consulted about the original grant.   (19.12.86)

WINTER CELEBRATION

Sitting at the traffic lights noting everything blurred by mist and gilded by a hidden street light was enough to remind me how beautiful are the trees in winter.

Do you remember back in the 1950's, when no Christmas card collection was complete without those expansive watercolours by Rowland Hilder? He had risen to be the most popular British artist alive.

His great rolling farmlands of rich brown earth between Beech clumps and stately Elms all flickering with light from the most English of winter skies had so much atmosphere.

So quietly they reassured that all was well; air, earth and water all painted with utmost assurance - and yet this was not part of a tradition in English art. Rowland Hilder's paintings were the first major celebration of the English countryside in winter. Only Turner has anything else to offer.

Also surprising is that Rowland Hilder did not turn naturally to this subject. He was our greatest marine artist, working among the boats and ships of the Thames estuary and around the English coast or over in Holland, but to support his family he undertook a daunting amount of commercial work. It was one of these commissions that created the first major Rowland Hilder winter landscape. Aware that this was new to the public the publicity practically told people to like it, and they certainly did.

The Garden of England was the ideal landscape and convenient for Hilder, living at Blackheath and sailing the Kent creeks. Soon, however, the war broke out and the Hilders moved, not to Kent but to Surrey, at Caterham. Not for long. Hilder was posted to Farnham Castle for camouflage training and the Hilders took a small house in West Street. Thus there are Surrey scenes in Hilder's work.

Once, out on exercises, there was a pause at Tilford, but long enough for Hilder to pencil across a lined page in his notebook a sketch of the adjacent farm. There, nestling among the trees, are the barn roofs and hay rick just waiting to be worked into one of his great paintings. Another notebook contains a study of the bole of a great cedar tree. He found that in the ground of Frensham Heights where his children were schooled. Over on the outskirts of Farnham he recorded High Mill as a rich snowscape. He had a very sharp eye for detail and could recreate all the everyday bustle of the dockside, but in his landscapes he omitted moving details that would detract from the atmosphere of the quiet calm.

(28.12.90)

KING GALLOPS ACROSS PAVEMENT

While the three kings marched from Christmas card to Christmas card across the bookshelf I got called out to see a very different king. Up the stairs, through the door and there was the giant king galloping his horse across nine square metres of bricks. To his right the porter called anxiously from his gatehouse; another nine square metres of bricks.

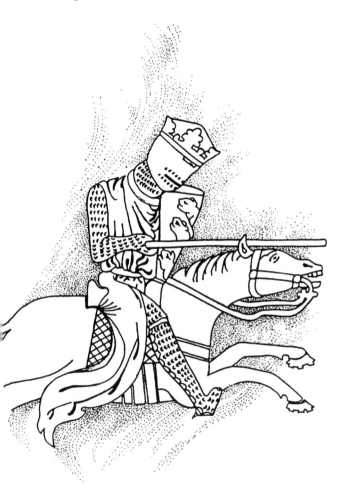

Chertsey artist Victor Spink was recreating giant versions of designs first drawn over 700 years ago. This had been the work of the Master of the Chertsey Tiles. His name is unknown. His supremacy is undisputed. Now, backed by Runnymede Borough Council, two designs are being enlarged about eight times and painted on to bricks to be set in the paving outside Chertsey Hall where everyone can see them.

"The Master of the Chertsey Tiles was the finest artist craftsman in this medium," enthused Victor, "and I want to show him to 20th century people."

It's been quite a job. The red background of the tiles has been recreated with special coloured concrete bricks. The soft golden slipware designs were being painted on with tinted road-marking paint. The effect is dramatic but not crude. The bricks have been selected for their colour variations and the paint variously tinted so that there is subtlety even in something so big and bold.

Sheets of paper lie all around on which can be seen Victor's shaded enlargements of the original designs. From these he cut stencils and so began the jigsaw tedium of fitting them all together, securing them in place, and dabbing through the paint.

"It's hard on your knees," he joked, with the sort of look that said it was no joke at all. The king's opinion was hidden behind his leather helmet. His adversary was missing. The companion isn't being recreated as it shows the death of Saladin and Christians killing Moslems would not be diplomatic at present.

Instead, Victor has chosen the only tile on which the Master showed architecture. It's the most intriguing tile, too, for while all his other work is in pure Gothic he drew on this one an old-fashioned building with Romanesque round-headed windows. Was this the view from his own window - out over an enclosure, past a great church to the boundary wall and the roof of a big building beyond? Is this the Chertsey Abbey complex? It's tempting to think it is, but we'll never know.

Early in the new year they'll be on display - for people to walk all over. Doesn't Victor mind that? "No! The Chertsey Tiles are a medium that goes underfoot. I feel very strongly about that. You usually see them on walls in museums."

"They'll look even better in the rain," he enthused and sprayed water on part of the design. Sure enough all the subtle reds and yellows glowed in the moisture.

There was still a lot of work for Victor and his assistant Miss Mandy Smith, to complete before the deadline at the end of Boxing Day. What a Christmas for them! Then I heard myself agreeing to help. Oh well, down with the pen, up with the brush but, oh dear, it's going to be hard on the knees! (29.12.89)

RIGHT: The Clock Jack at
       Abinger Hammer.

BOTTOM RIGHT: Sculpture from
              Guildford Cathedral.

BOTTOM: Joan Brocas from her
        memorial brass in
        Peper Harow Church.

BELOW: Detail from illustration
       to a feature on introducing
       children to Surrey heritage.

INDEX

PEOPLE

INDEX

PLACES